THE STORY OF *Your* LIFE

MATTHEW WEST
ANGELA THOMAS

HARVEST HOUSE PUBLISHERS

EUGENE, OREGON

Cover by Pixel Peach Studio, Austin, Texas

Angela Thomas: Published in association with BrandWaves LLC

Matthew West: Published in association with the literary agency of Fedd & Company, Inc., 606 Flamingo Blvd., Austin, TX 78734.

THE STORY OF YOUR LIFE
Copyright © 2011 by Matthew West and Angela Thomas
Published by Harvest House Publishers
Eugene, Oregon 97402
www.harvesthousepublishers.com

Library of Congress Cataloging-in-Publication Data
West, Matthew.
  The story of your life / Matthew West and Angela Thomas.
    p. cm.
  ISBN 978-0-7369-4398-7 (pbk.)
  ISBN 978-0-7369-4399-4 (eBook)
  1. Christian life. 2. Storytelling—Religious aspects—Christianity. 3. Christian biography. I.
Thomas, Angela, 1962- II. Title.
  BV4501.3.W426 2011
  242'.4—dc22
                                                                          2011007500

I want to dedicate this book to the 10,000 people who opened a window to their worlds to me. You are the proof that we all have a story to tell. This is your book.

Acknowledgments

I would like to thank my manager (and brother), Joel West, for believing in my dream to extend my writing beyond the confines of a three-minute song. Thanks to my girls, Emily, Lulu, and Delaney, for constant love, patience, and support. To my mom and dad—you told me someday I'd be writing books. You're the proof that kids should never doubt their parents! Thanks to Angela Thomas for teaming up with me and lending your gift of words to this project. Thanks to Esther Fedorkevich, Terry Glaspey, and the Harvest House family for your belief in the power of a story. Thanks to God, the author of every story. And thanks to you for taking this journey of discovering the power of a story with me.

A very special thanks to Matthew. Your idea to invite people to share their stories with you was both tender and brilliant. I love the songs you wrote, and I'm so grateful you invited me to share in those stories for this devotional. Thanks to Harvest House, Terry Glaspey, and Gene Skinner for all your help and encouragement on this journey together. Thanks to my family—Scott, Taylor, Grayson, William, and AnnaGrace—for the loving patience you have given while I do just one more thing. But most of all, thank You, Jesus. May every word we have written give glory and honor to the greater story of Your love.

CONTENTS

INTRODUCTION

At first, spending two months hidden away in a Tennessee cabin seemed to be the perfect escape from the world while I wrote songs for a new record. Turns out, I took the whole world to that cabin with me. I asked people to send me their stories, and they did. Stories came pouring in by the thousands from every state in the United States and from 20 different countries around the world. The response was overwhelming, and I quickly sensed that something special was about to take place.

The idea was simple, or so I thought. My plan was to turn the microphone around. See, as a songwriter, I typically use the medium of music as a way of telling my story. I write about the world the way I see it, finding inspiration from personal experience. But over the years, I have been continually drawn to the stories of people who have listened to my music and then sent me e-mail or Facebook messages or met me after a show. Every time someone opens windows for me to see inside his or her world, I am awakened to the thought that each of our lives is telling a story. And so I wondered, what if instead of writing my story, I became the messenger and wrote songs inspired by the stories of other people's lives? I have found that "What if...?" can be a dangerous question to ask. It was this question that led this city boy to the solitude of a cabin in the woods.

Henri Nouwen refers to solitude as a "furnace of transformation." My time inside those wooden walls fit his description. For two months, my world was absolutely rocked by the stories I read. Stories of victory and stories of heartbreak. Stories of redemption and stories of tragedy. Stories that made me laugh and stories that made me cry. These stories moved me. They opened my eyes to see the world around me in a new light, and I believe they will do the same for you.

Shortly after my time in the cabin, I was scheduled to perform at a conference in Austin, Texas. There I met author and speaker Angela Thomas. During my show, I shared about the journey I had recently embarked on. After the event was over, Angela came up to me and said, "You need to write a book about this, and I would love to write it with you!" Angela's enthusiasm that day confirmed what had already been stirring in my heart, and I believe God brought the two of us together to write this book you are now holding in your hands. Her unique gift of communication and her inspiring knowledge of Scripture have been key pieces of this puzzle. Together we have collected 52 powerful real-life stories that will inspire you, challenge you, and even change the way you see the world. Along with each story, we have written a devotion that further explores its power as well as God's plan for the story of your life.

In a way, I guess I'm bringing the cabin to you. And I hope as you read these stories, you will be challenged, inspired, and changed the way I was. But most of all, I hope that as you read this book, you will find yourself taking a deeper look at your own story—past, present, and future. May you join thousands of others by living every day knowing that the story of your life is a story worth telling.

1

WHO IS THE AUTHOR OF YOUR STORY?

From Lajos...

I grew up in Communist Hungary and escaped in 1987 at age 21. I went to a refugee camp as an atheist who mocked Christians, and 18 months later I came out of it turning my life over to Christ. It was a trying, dramatic, and sometimes traumatic experience. But in the middle of what should have been my most hopeless days and nights, I could not deny the overwhelming feeling that I was not alone and the peace that came along with it.

I went to Canada in 1988. Starting a new life in a new country as a 23-year-old was truly challenging. Without my newly found faith, I probably could not have done it. Now I am following Christ and serving Him by going on mission trips. I want the world to know there is a God, a God who is with us in our darkest moments.

The heavens declare the glory of God; the skies proclaim the work of his hands (Psalm 19:1).

The Son is the image of the invisible God, the firstborn over all creation. For in him all things were created: things in heaven and on earth, visible and invisible, whether thrones or powers of rulers or authorities; all things have been created through him and for him. He is before all things, and in him all things hold together (Colossians 1:15-17).

…fixing our eyes on Jesus, the author and perfecter of faith… (Hebrews 12:2 NASB).

Matthew Responds…

Who is the author of your story? How did you get here? Do you see the world as nothing more than one big coincidence after another? Did the oceans just tell themselves they could go only so far? Did the sun just appear out of nowhere? What about all the billions of stars in the galaxies or the intricate design of a human life? Is there an answer for all these questions?

When your eyes see a majestic snowcapped mountain climbing a mile high in the Rockies, does the experience leave you awestruck and amazed? When you hold a newborn baby in your arms, are you filled with wonder as you touch the tiny hands and toes and ears? When you witness a great big world with billions of people moving in billions of directions, does your heart scream, "This can't be mere coincidence! This could not be the work of human hands! There's no way this all just happened!"

Even the English astronomer Sir Fred Hoyle concluded, "The chance that higher life forms might have emerged in this way is comparable with the chance that 'a tornado sweeping through a junk yard might assemble a Boeing 747 from the materials therein.'"*

Sadly, more and more people are choosing the former way of thinking. In fact, many studies and polls report that atheism is on the rise both in America and around the world. This really should come as no surprise in a society that places so much emphasis on self-sufficiency. Nike prompted us, "Just Do It." Burger King invited us, "Have It Your Way." Apple Computers promised their products would give us "The Power to Be Your Best."

---

* Cited in J.P. Moreland, *The Creation Hypothesis* (Downers Grove: IVP Books, 1994), 273.

In our world, all signs point to the notion that you and I are the ones who write the stories of our lives. And so people are choosing to believe there is nothing to believe in. Atheists believe there is no God. And to believe there is no God is to believe we are the authors of our own stories. Yet how can we be the authors of a story we never created? You were not the one who came up with the idea to create you. The decision of whether to believe in God is the foundation that every soul will build its story upon. The story of your life is being written every moment of every day, even as you read this right now. The question you must ask is, who is holding the pen?

In his book *The Purpose Driven Life*, Rick Warren begins his very first chapter by establishing where we must first look if we are to find a story with true purpose.

> You must begin with God, your Creator. You exist only because God wills that you exist. You were made *by* God and *for* God—and until you understand that, life will never make sense. It is only in God we discover our origin, our identity, our meaning, our purpose, our significance, and our destiny. Every other path leads to a dead end.*

Warren goes on to tell the story of Russian novelist, Andrei Bitov who had a similar experience to our story of Lajos.

> Andrei…grew up under an atheistic Communist regime. But God got his attention one dreary day. He recalls, "In my twenty-seventh year, while riding the metro in Leningrad (now St. Petersburg) I was overcome with a despair so great that life seemed to stop at once, preempting the future entirely, let alone any meaning. Suddenly, all by itself, a phrase appeared: Without God life makes no sense. Repeating it in astonishment, I rode the phrase up like a moving staircase, got out of the metro and walked into God's light."†

---

* Rick Warren, *The Purpose-Driven Life* (Grand Rapids: Zondervan, 2007).

† Warren, *The Purpose-Driven Life*, 21.

There it is. Without God life makes no sense. Without God our stories have no meaning, no purpose. We live, we die, and that's it. Our stories end when we die. Oh, what a sad existence if this is true. I once wrote a lyric in a song called "The World Needs a Savior" that reads, "Atheists, there are no atheists when the plane's going down and you're crying out for one more chance." I wrote that line thinking about the reality that when people face crisis, they reach out for help. When our nation, which fights for separation of church and state, fell victim to the terrorist attacks on 9/11, we came together to pray.

I remember something my mom often did when I was a kid and we were in the car. Anytime she was forced to slam on her brakes or swerve out of the way to avoid an accident, her knee-jerk reaction was to stretch her arm out across whoever was sitting in the front seat, either my brother or me, and shout a prayer: "Jesus, help us!" My mom is a praying woman. She always has been, both in times of triumph and times of crisis. She knows whom she can call upon. She knows the all-knowing and all-powerful God. She knows that God hears us when we call out to Him in a whisper of praise or a cry for help.

Whom do you call out to in times of crisis? Lajos was once convinced God did not exist. But in the middle of his loneliest, most desperate hour, this "atheist who mocked Christians" cried out to Jesus. "I could not deny the overwhelming feeling that I was not alone and the peace that came along with it," he said as the undeniable presence of our Creator turned this atheist into a believer. Lajos handed over the pen right then and there, choosing to make God the author of his story.

Maybe you are thinking, "This doesn't apply to me. I believe in God. I'm no atheist." Well, let me leave you with this one question. Who is really holding the pen? It is possible to believe in God, go to church, tithe, and do all the things Christians do without fully submitting the story of your life to the true "author and finisher" of our faith. It is a daily struggle to determine who holds the pen, but surrendering our stories to the One who "holds all things together" is the only true way for the stories of our lives to be filled with meaning and purpose.

2

THE OLDER BROTHER

From Webster...

Until recently, I've compared my life with that of the prodigal son's older brother. I always slaved away, following rules and regulations to the best of my ability, and whenever I failed, either I would be overwhelmed with guilt and shame or I would make exceptions for myself in my own mind. Never knowing how much my Father loved me, I tried to do His bidding with everything I had. I went to church every Sunday, attended Sunday school, went to church camps...I did everything right, or so I thought. I grew up without the love of the Father—not because it wasn't there, but because I was caught up trying to please Him. I bet a lot of people have grown up in church doing everything right in their own minds but not really having a relationship with the Father.

Meanwhile, the older son was in the field. When he came near the house, he heard music and dancing. So he called one of the servants and asked him what was going on. "Your brother has come," he replied, "and your father has killed the fattened calf because he has him back safe and sound."

The older brother became angry and refused to go in. So his

*father went out and pleaded with him. But he answered his
father, "Look! All these years I've been slaving for you and never
disobeyed your orders. Yet you never gave me even a young goat
so I could celebrate with my friends. But when this son of yours
who has squandered your property with prostitutes comes home,
you kill the fattened calf for him!"*

*"My son," the father said, "you are always with me, and
everything I have is yours"* (Luke 15:25-31).

Angela Responds…

You remember the story of the prodigal son. A son asked his father
for his inheritance. Because the father loved his son so much, he gave
his son what he had asked for. The son promptly went off to a distant
country and squandered everything his father had given to him. One
day, broke and hungry, the son "came to his senses" and decided to
go home. When the prodigal came home, the father threw a great big
party to celebrate his lost son's return.

But the prodigal son had an older brother. He was the one who
stayed home, never did anything rebellious, and worked faithfully on
his father's farm. And the day his little brother came home, the older
brother got mad. His real heart seemed to come out that day—arro-
gant, haughty, judgmental, and angry that his younger brother received
forgiveness. The older brother completely missed the point.

The older brother had been with his father every day, and still he
had missed it. He had missed having a relationship with him. He had
missed the privilege of enjoying everything that belonged to his father.
And that night, he missed the celebration. Maybe he stomped off to
his room and slammed his door, missing the music, the dancing, and
especially the beauty of his father's love.

I am sure there is an older brother inside me. It's the part of me
that forgets the relationship I can have with my heavenly Father, forgets the lavish inheritance I have been given every day, forgets that my
Father's love reaches past my judgment and my arrogance to reach any
who would return to Him. And in my forgetfulness, I can miss the celebration of that love.

Maybe today, you and I, we can remember how big and deep and high is the Father's love for us. Maybe we can remember moment to moment to enjoy His presence. Day after day, He is faithful to keep all His promises to us. This is a Father we can have a relationship with, a Father more concerned with our hearts than with the rules we checked off our lists today. And maybe if we remember who He is and how much He loves, we will enjoy more music in our lives and especially more dancing.

How great is the Father's love for us. This day, don't forget to remember and rejoice!

3

A CHARACTER IN SOMEONE ELSE'S STORY

From Stefanie...

My chemistry partner in high school invited me to church my junior year. I gave my life to the Lord and started working on my family. My best friend, brother, sister, mother, and father all were saved within the next year and a half. I went off to Bible college, but God was still working on others back home. My grandparents gave their hearts to the Lord while I was away at school.

Last year my cousin got cancer, and while he was sick, he gave his heart to the Lord. He passed away in May, and his parents were devastated. I knew they would either turn away from God or walk toward Him. Now, on any given Sunday you will find them sitting next to my family at church. And this is all because there was a flame given to me and everyone wanted a flame of their own. It has been six years since I was invited to church, and now I am a pastor with my husband. God has only just begun His work in my life!

From Shannon...

I attended my ten-year reunion, and a friend asked if he could tell me a story. About eight years ago, he had planned on committing suicide. He decided to look through his yearbook to see if there might be anyone who would miss him. As he was reading the words that people had written to him there, he noticed what I had written: "Edward, I hope that one day you know God the way that I do." Then he thought about me and the life he had seen me live since way back in first grade, and he thought, "Yeah, maybe she does have something I need." So he told God if He could give him what I have, then he wanted it. Now he's married, has two kids, and is a leader at his church, and he just wanted to say thanks. He said I had made a difference in his life whether I knew it or not.

You are the salt of the earth...You are the light of the world. A town built on a hill cannot be hidden. Neither do people light a lamp and put it under a bowl. Instead they put it on its stand, and it gives light to everyone in the house. In the same way, let your light shine before others, that they may see your good deeds and glorify your Father in heaven (Matthew 5:13-16).

The harvest is plentiful but the workers are few. Ask the Lord of the harvest, therefore, to send out workers into his harvest field (Matthew 9:37-38).

You will be my witnesses in Jerusalem, and in all Judea and Samaria, and to the end of the earth (Acts 1:8).

Matthew Responds...

Notice a similarity in today's stories. Neither of these people came to a personal faith in Christ after hearing an outspoken Bible thumper who pointed a finger in their faces and made them painfully aware of their pending eternity in hell if they did not choose to turn from their wicked ways. Neither was led to faith in Christ by a licensed counselor or energetic evangelist. These people were reached by simple, loving acts of kindness from everyday people who chose to daily live out their stories in a Christlike way. I love reading these stories because they remind me that when we make the choice to remain faithful to God's leading in our lives, we never know when, where, or how He might choose to use us in someone else's story.

The Christian community talks a lot about sharing our faith and witnessing. But often, this act of sharing faith is made out to be a formal conversation with someone about Jesus, the kind that ends in reciting a sinner's prayer. And although that very well may be something that can happen in time, we must daily remember that we are sharing our faith (or lack of it) long before we ever sit down and have "the talk" with someone.

Because of my ministry as a singer and writer, I actually find myself sharing my faith in a structured way, speaking to audiences from the stage every night about the importance of a personal relationship with Jesus. Over time I have noticed a tendency in my own spirit to sort of check off the "share your faith" box because of my job, and then I shut down a little, acting as if that one hour on stage lets me off the hook for the other 23 hours in my day. I'll give you an example.

I spend a regrettable amount of time in airports. These places bring out the absolute worst in me. Security lines, delayed flights, occasionally less-than-friendly flight attendants...airports are pretty much my least favorite places to be (just ask my road manager). They are where I come the closest to becoming a diva. And on most trips, by the time I get settled into my seat on the plane, I'm absolutely exhausted, wanting nothing more than to attempt to sleep awkwardly with my forehead smashed against the window. Over the years I have mastered the art of making sure whoever is seated next to me knows I have absolutely no interest in chitchat. Here are a few tricks of the trade.

1. Under no circumstance are you to make eye contact.

2. Pretend to be really busy, or have headphones on so you can't hear if a person attempts to engage in conversation.

3. Wear some type of hooded clothing that you can pull over your head, thus creating a physical barrier between you and a potential privacy invader. (This also makes you look a bit creepy and unapproachable.)

4. And finally, if all else fails, reach for the barf bag. No one wants to talk to someone who looks like he might lose his lunch at the first sign of turbulence.

I wish I were joking, but I am embarrassed to say I have gone to these lengths to avoid entering in to someone's story! I have a feeling I'm not the only one. Ever take a different route to your desk at work to avoid someone you don't like talking to? Or how about pretending not to see the homeless person in front of you holding a sign? At times, we are all tempted to avoid entering into someone else's story for fear of what may be required of us.

But every single day, God not only calls us into our own stories but also invites us to become characters in the stories of other people's lives. It happens when you say good morning to your spouse. It happens when you see your boss on Monday. It happens when you pass the new kid in the hallway at school or even when you think no one is watching. We can easily underestimate and often overlook the potential impact of these daily encounters with the world around us, but the way we handle such encounters can mean a world of difference for those who are watching.

As these two stories showed, your actions can have as much influence as your words—maybe even more. That is why the Bible instructs us, "Let us not love with words or speech but with actions and in truth" (1 John 3:18). D.L. Moody wrote, "Of one hundred men, one will read the Bible; the ninety-nine will read the Christian." I know people who seem to see every encounter with someone as a chance to show him or her Jesus. By my airport confession, we have already established that I am not one of those people. But I'm trying. I ask God to give me the discernment to know when to join someone else's story, the wisdom to know how, and the willingness to follow through every time He calls me to. Try praying that same prayer today. Pray that when people "read" you, their stories will be touched by the love of Jesus that you display.

4

CHOSEN

From Linda...

Chosen—twice.

I was adopted to a family that God wanted to touch with His love. My adoptive mother prayed for a child to fill the void of the one-day-old child she lost. God has had His hand in my life. I didn't find out I was adopted until I was already married and with my first child. You would think that maybe I would have some resentment, but God placed a spirit of peace in my heart.

Around the same time I found out I was adopted, God called me to His eternal family, and I was chosen again—not just from the cry of a mother's heart but from the heart of God. I am now 50, and God has been so faithful to me. I have been searching for my bio-logical mother, and I am very close to that reconciliation. I believe God is going to bring healing and forgiveness to my birth mother.

The lesson from my life is that we are not our own. God created us for His purpose. "From one man he made every nation of men, that they should inhabit the whole earth; and he determined the times set for them and the exact places where they should live" (Acts 17:26).

I hope that all women who have given their children up for adop-tion can believe that God is with those children and has a plan for them. I give God glory and praise for the life He has given me and for including me in His plan.

What I am saying is that as long as an heir is underage, he is no different from a slave, although he owns the whole estate. The heir is subject to guardians and trustees until the time set by his father. So also, when we were underage, we were in slavery under the elemental spiritual forces of the world. But when the set time had fully come, God sent his Son, born of a woman, born under the law, to redeem those under the law, that we might receive adoption to sonship. Because you are his sons, God sent the Spirit of his Son into our hearts, the Spirit who calls out, "Abba, Father." So you are no longer a slave, but God's child; and since you are his child, God has made you also an heir (Galatians 4:1-7).

Angela Responds...

Many people on this earth have experienced the life-changing story of adoption. Eight years ago, my brother and sister-in-law gave our family the privilege of participating in the beauty of their story. That snowy winter, they flew to an orphanage in Russia and chose their son, our youngest nephew, Cole. They were travel-weary when the whole family met them at the airport, but I will never forget the tears on every face as we met the little baby boy safely sleeping in his earthly father's arms. My brother was perfectly his daddy, my sister-in-law, his mommy.

But even more spectacular is the eternity-changing story of being adopted into the family of God. Before our adoption, each one of us lives as an orphan in this world. Without an eternal home, without a forever family, without the privileges of our Father's inheritance. But God sent His Son, Jesus, so that we might receive His plan of adoption, becoming sons and daughters of the King of Glory.

Spiritual adoption is an act of God whereby believers become members of God's family with all the privileges and obligations of family membership. When we have been adopted into the family, God, who is holy and sovereign, becomes our loving Father. We are His. We belong to Him. The Bible goes on to teach that when we become children of God, He sends the Spirit of His Son into our hearts so that we can call out to God, "*Abba*," which means "daddy."

To belong to the family of God means we are no longer slaves to our sin or slaves to the limitations of this world. We have been made heirs with full family rights and privileges.

At a dinner party one night, two of my girlfriends both told the table of guests they had been adopted into families as babies. One of the adopted women turned to the other and asked, "Did you buy your parents a gift when you graduated from college?"

The other adopted woman said, "Why, yes I did. Did you?"

"Of course," the other responded. "I was just so grateful for all they have given to me."

"Me too," the first agreed.

The rest of us sheepishly sat at the table, completely convicted. It had never occurred to any of us to give a thank-you gift to our parents for our education. We had all taken our family privilege for granted. Our two adopted friends had lived lives of gratitude for having been chosen.

What if every day we remembered what God has done for us? What if we reminded ourselves, "I am adopted into the family. I belong to God. I am His child, and nothing—nothing!—will ever change that. I will be with Him forever. Undeserving as I am, His inheritance is mine. I am safe. I am set apart. I am forgiven. Oh, glory, I am loved!"

And then, what if from our gratefulness, we lived this one life as a gift back to God? Our passionate lives of purpose would be our souls' greatest thank you. We would act as if we belong to the family. We would love like children of the Father, give as has been given to us, serve as Jesus has served.

Maybe this world would take notice of our lives, and we would have the great privilege of telling them about our Father, the One who adopts the orphans of this world. And then, wouldn't it be something if they were able to look at us and say, "Ah yes, I see the family resemblance"?

5

GOD DOESN'T MAKE MISTAKES

From Kristin...

I've been battling with depression for a long time, and in 2005 I tried to take my life. Later, after I began healing, I wrote a poem that describes how I felt and what I experienced.

> Can You feel my pain?
> Can You sense the agony?
> Can You see the tears through the pouring rain?
> Lord, was I just a mistake?
>
> Don't want to be a memory.
> Just let me soar with the wind.
> Never to be seen or heard again.
> No strings attached.
> Lord, just set me free, and I'll love You anyway.
>
> I tried to take my life away.
> Woke up in disgrace.
> I wanted to see You face-to-face.
> Lord, I was Your only mistake.
>
> Still, I'll love You anyway.
> When it's Your will, I'll see Your face.

Until that day, I'll dream away
And live my life on Your love and my faith.

As for God, his way is perfect (Psalm 18:30).

Through him all things were made; without him nothing was made that has been made (John 1:3).

[Nothing] will be able to separate us from the love of God that is in Christ Jesus (Romans 8:39).

Angela Responds...

Jesus said in the book of John, "In this world you will have trouble" (John 16:33). No matter how many years you have lived, I bet you have already known enough trouble in this world. It comes to everyone. No one is exempt from the hard things that happen to the living.

When you and I face trouble or heartache or pain, we can begin to focus on the darkness in our lives and miss the never-failing presence of God. After enough rejection and disappointment, we can even begin to doubt God, wondering if He's made a big mistake, wondering if He has forgotten about our trouble and our pain. But it's the accuser who whispers those lies. Satan is the one who calls your life worthless. He is the one who makes you doubt. Satan is the one who wants you to believe your life and God's ways are mistakes. When you are already suffering the troubles of this world, Satan can step in with his lies and make things even worse. My friend says, "The devil shouts; God whispers." Maybe all you've heard lately are the shouts.

Could it be that today you need to know our God is perfect in all His ways? And God, in His perfect character, can never be other than He is. God can never be anything less than perfect. He has given you this life because He has a plan and a purpose for you. His decision to give you life was a perfect decision. He did not make a mistake about where you should be born. He is not mistaken about His love for you or the future He has planned for you. You may have made some mistakes in your lifetime, but God did not make a mistake about you. He believed in the beauty of your life before you ever were.

Jesus goes on in that same passage to give us an important promise: "In this world you will have trouble. But take heart! I have overcome the world."

Maybe you need to hear that Jesus, the Son of God, is the overcomer. That means that regardless of what you face today, Jesus can show you what to do. He can teach you how to walk through the next few minutes, the next day, and the next year. He is the answer to all that concerns you. He is the way when you are lost. He is the light for your darkness. He is the bondage breaker and the sin forgiver. He is the answer, and in Him, every single one of us has hope.

Someone has said, "When you don't know what to do or where to turn, just do the next right thing." Maybe the next right thing is to bow your head and turn your heart toward God. Maybe the next right thing is to call someone who can help you find your way. Maybe the next right thing is to finally believe in a perfect God who doesn't make mistakes. He is the same God who can take the pieces of your life and make them into more than you could dream for yourself. He is the perfect God with perfect ways. He is the One who longs to care for your heart.

No matter how this world has made you feel about yourself, no matter the disappointments you've known, these truths remain: Our God is perfect in all His ways. He made you on purpose without a mistake. He longs to work in your disappointment to bring good from your pain. And nothing—nothing, my friend—can ever separate you from His deep, abiding love.

If you need help today, if your thoughts are cloudy and suicide feels like an option to you, please pick up the phone and call one of the National Suicide Prevention numbers listed below.* Someone is there waiting to talk to you this very minute, waiting to tell you about the God who never makes mistakes.

---

* 1-800-SUICIDE (1-800-784-2433), 1-800-273-TALK (1-800-273-8255)

6

A STORY JUDGED BY ITS COVER

From Michelle...

Have you ever felt the pain of middle school? I have through my son, Conner.

There are many things most people do not know about him. He was born premature and has had an uphill climb ever since. He has a learning disability and struggles to learn on a daily basis. He thinks of himself as stupid. However, he works harder than anyone I know.

He is just looking for a friend who will accept him as he is. Someone to hang with and do things with on the weekends. Doesn't everyone deserve a true friend?

He wants a girlfriend so bad that he lets popular girls say mean things to him on Facebook. His profile says he has 255 friends, but they are friends who will not even say hi back when he passes them in the hallway at school. Nevertheless, he is so proud of all those so-called friends.

Conner is my inspiration because through all of the painful moments, he still has such empathy for people and can forgive in a heartbeat. Sometimes I wonder how he can get up each morning, put a smile on his face, and be positive when he has so many negative things going on around him.

I always tell him that God has something special waiting for him because of all the struggles he has been through since his birth.

Humble yourselves, therefore, under God's mighty hand, that he may lift you up in due time (1 Peter 5:6).

But many who are first will be last, and many who are last will be first (Matthew 19:30).

Matthew Responds...

"Have you ever felt the pain of middle school?"

Why, yes, I have! Reading the first line of this story made me feel as though someone had found my junior-high diary, and my mind suddenly drifted back to a picture of an overweight sixth grader on the day he learned the hard way that "Matt" rhymes with "fat." Looking back, I'm fairly certain one of the reasons for my husky build as a child was my love for all things sweet.

This sweet tooth was undoubtedly passed on to me by my father, God love him. When I was a kid, his idea of exercise was taking a bike ride...all the way to Dairy Queen! Then, after indulging in a tasty treat, we would call my mom for a ride home. She would pick us up, and we would throw our bicycles in the back of that old station wagon. So, yeah, I felt the pain of middle school. The crazy thing is, even though I don't get picked on anymore and I grew out of that phase in my life long ago, I can see how those harsh words played into some of the insecurities I carry with me even today. At times, I struggle with being overly self-conscious about my appearance, and I can catch myself being way too concerned about what people think of me or whether they like me.

What about you? Ever felt the pain of middle school? High school? College? The workplace? It doesn't matter who we are, where we come from, or where in our lives we are now; the world can turn a cold shoulder to anyone anytime without any warning. It will go out of its way at times to make you feel unlovable, disqualified, or just not good enough. Yes, at some point someone may judge your story by the cover, making you feel worthless. It's that nasty rumor spread by a so-called friend at church. The degrading put-downs from a father who never helped to build your self-esteem. The negativity of a spouse who seems to think he or she should always bring your dreams down to size. Seeds of insecurity can grow into an unhealthy and tainted view of yourself if you allow them to take root.

Michelle called Conner an inspiration because he forgives those kids who make fun of him. Conner reminds me of Joseph in the Bible. Joseph's brothers hated and bullied their younger brother to such an extent that they betrayed him and sold him into slavery. "They hated him and could not speak a kind word to him" (Genesis 37:4). But God had bigger plans for Joseph. Little did his brothers know that one day God would raise Joseph up to a high place of power and they would bow before him. God used all the bad that had happened in his life, and in the end, Joseph was able to forgive his brothers, who had bullied him so badly.

God has a plan for Conner. He has a plan for you too. Sure, Joseph spent most of his youth in slavery in Egypt, but God raised him up. He will raise you up as well. "Humble yourselves...that he may lift you up in due time." He is raising up Conner these days, and people are starting to take notice that he really is an awesome young man.

After reading Michelle's story about her son, Conner, I kept thinking to myself, "I want to meet this kid." On an August afternoon, I had the opportunity to do just that. My band and I had a show in Michigan, about two hours from where Conner and his family live. So instead of driving straight to our concert, we made a slight detour and pulled the tour bus up in front of his family's home. I knocked on their door and had the chance to meet Michelle and Conner face-to-face. I told Michelle how much her story inspired me, and played a song I wrote called "To Me" that was inspired by the heart of this mom who wishes her son could see just how special he really is.

After spending the morning in the family's living room, I invited

Conner to join the band for the day. He rode with us on the tour bus all the way to our concert, and we spent the day together. I will never forget introducing him to an audience of 12,000 people at the festival. He walked onstage, and the entire crowd rose to their feet, cheering for Conner. He was the star of the show, and for a moment, all the bullying was a million miles away.

Later in the year, Fox News heard about Conner and invited us to New York to tell his story on national television. God is now raising up Conner with a timely message in light of the many tragic bullying stories that are surfacing.

Stories of kids like Alex, a boy who was being bullied at his middle school. He came home from school one day and announced to his parents, "I found out it's not cool to be smart." Little did his parents know that Alex would take his own life at the age of 16, leaving one final note to his parents saying he was sorry. He added, "But I can't take it anymore."

Maya Angelou wrote, "I have learned that people will forget what you said, people will forget what you did, but people will never forget how you made them feel." Next time you are tempted to judge someone's story by the cover, remember Conner, remember Joseph, and remember Alex. And if you should find yourself being bullied or judged, may you be quick to forgive just as Conner did, and may you be quick to remember that God will raise you up in due time, just as He raised up Joseph.

The story of your life goes much deeper than the cover. The author of your story will surely make your life a must-read from cover to cover.

7

MY SINGLE-MOM LIFE

Angela's Story...

As a thirtysomething mom to four young children, I couldn't believe my story was being interrupted by separation and divorce. I grew up thinking I would be able to write my own story. You know, make a plan, work the plan, and then live the life you had planned. What I now understand is that you can make a plan and do the very best you can, but then life comes up to meet you with all kinds of twists and turns, many of them painful.

I believed I would never use certain words to describe my life. *Divorce* was one of the big ones. I was a Christian, committed to the principles of lasting marriage. I was raised by parents who have now been married nearly 50 years. I guess I just thought that commitment was a family trait we would pass down from one generation to the next. Divorce was something that happened to other people, not us.

And then I was divorced.

I became an unprepared single mom to my two daughters and two sons. The first three years were the most miserable, embarrassing, shameful years I have ever known. I had officially become a broken woman with a broken home and broken dreams. And I guess, truth be told, I thought my story was irretrievably broken as well. For some reason, I had a sinking feeling that I would have to limp along the rest of my life—wounded, hanging my head, and forever embarrassed about the way my story turned out.

Before my marriage and divorce, I had known God personally, and I had known a lot about Him. I had a seminary degree to prove it. But as it turns out, I didn't really know the depth of God's love for me at all. I had the impression that God backed away from broken people, people who sin, and people who suffer the consequences of their choices. I was wrong. Hallelujah, I was wrong. You see, God leans in. He moves closer. He comes to heal the broken, and He came to heal me. More importantly, God is healing my children, whom I love so much. And He's doing it all for His glory, not mine.

Two years ago, my four children and I were married to the best man I have ever met on this earth, Scott Pharr. Who could have believed there was a man to love me and my kids? My God did. Who would think of sending a man I've known since I was 16 to soothe all my issues of trust? Same God. Who could make a man with no children fall in love with someone else's kids as if they were his very own? Our really big God, who is able.

My story is not one I would have signed up for. Matter of fact, I would have run from this story if someone had offered it to me. But God, according to His grace and mercy, is writing new chapters to this single-mom story to show off His love.

And I pray that you, being rooted and established in love, may have power, together with all the Lord's holy people, to grasp how wide and long and high and deep is the love of Christ, and to know this love that surpasses knowledge—that you may be filled to the measure of all fullness of God (Ephesians 3:17-19).

Angela Responds...

The Bible is clear—God is mysterious. We know Him in part, and we understand in part. But knowing the fullness of God's love—its depth and height and width and length—will take us forever. His love for us surpasses knowledge. With every page of our stories, we are learning new truths about the measure of God's love for us.

While we live on this earth, we will endure trials, disappointment, pain, and sometimes just the dumb mistakes we have made. And many days, people on this earth can make us feel as if we will always be broken. Maybe you have checked the divorced box enough times and have begun to believe that's the way God sees you too. Or maybe all you can remember are your mistakes, and now you believe that's all God remembers about you.

I love knowing that God is able to do immeasurably more than broken people can ask or imagine. Did you know that? We, the broken, the embarrassed, and the ashamed, do not have to stay the way we are now. Our God is a rescuing God. He moves toward those who need His mercy. He heals the wounds we place in His hands. He takes our broken stories and writes new chapters according to His power and for His glory because of His Son, Christ Jesus.

Is your life broken too? Maybe you're living a story that hasn't turned out the way you'd always hoped. Will you trust that God is plotting more for you than you can ask or imagine? This day, God is already at work in your broken places, your broken heart, and even your broken home. He is the healing you need, the hope you long for, the rewriter of broken stories.

Sometimes we think our little stories are all there is. May God show each one of us that our stories are parts of His greater story. Over and over, God wants to show the world that He rescues those who can't save themselves. He restores the lives others renounced. He forgives the sin we can't make clean. He gives the sad and downtrodden a new life in Him. He finds the lost and sets their feet on new paths. He gives hope to those who have given up.

Our God is a great God. Oh, that we could finally understand how wide and long and high and deep is the love of Christ for each one of us!

8

ANYTHING IS POSSIBLE

From Wendy...

I spent 32 years in a destructive, downward spiral. I used to be convinced there was no way out. After my mom died, I found myself at my lowest point. I became pregnant unexpectedly and then ended up having to deliver my daughter while I was in jail. As you can imagine, this was my rock bottom.

But at a time when my life seemed the most hopeless, I found God, and He turned my life around. I found hope like I never had before, and I will never lose it again. In just six short years, I purchased my own house, I went back to school and got my bachelor's in counseling psychology, and I am a single mother to the most beautiful little girl ever. She has no doubt that God comes first, and I pray she never has to repeat my life. It hasn't been easy. But I know that if God can save someone like me, anything is possible!

Now to him who is able to do immeasurably more than all we ask or imagine, according to his power that is at work within us, to him be glory in the church and in Christ Jesus throughout all generations, forever and ever! Amen (Ephesians 3:20-21).

Matthew Responds...

My daughter came home from kids' church one Sunday morning singing a new song she learned in class. And when she learns a new song, she wears it out! The term "broken record" would apply (if anyone even knew what a record was anymore). All the way home she sang, "JESUS, YOU'RE MY SUPERHERO! JESUS, YOU'RE MY SUPERHERO!" She sang it so loud, I'm pretty sure all the cars on the road could hear her.

We sure love our superheroes, don't we? From comic books to action figures to box-office smashes, the world seems to have a fascination with the idea of a larger-than-life, good-versus-evil, save-the-day character who specializes in doing the impossible. Superhero franchises are among some of the biggest earners at the box office, with *Spider-man 3* bringing in $1.11 billion and *The Dark Knight* (the fifth in the Batman series) earning a whopping $1.45 billion.

"Faster than a speeding bullet, more powerful than a locomotive, and able to leap buildings in a single bound..."

But even our favorite fictitious figures have their limitations. These seemingly indestructible heroes have their flaws. Superman's notorious weakness? Kryptonite. Batman needed a sidekick, Robin. And the Incredible Hulk? What a temper! The guy couldn't even keep his shirt on.

So where can we turn to find a bona fide hero? A savior who *really* does the impossible? Well, come to think of it, perhaps that was more than just a catchy little tune my daughter was singing on the way home from church. There really *is* only One who is big enough, strong enough, and relentless enough to do the impossible every time.

Just ask Wendy. Anyone would have looked at her situation and quickly called her a lost cause. This woman hit such a low point that she had to give birth in jail! I confess, when I got to that part of her story, I was thinking to myself, "Another sad story of a hopeless cause." Not in a million years did I see what was coming next in Wendy's story! But Wendy discovered firsthand that our perfectly impossible circumstances are no match for our perfectly capable Savior. "I am the LORD...is anything too hard for me?" (Jeremiah 32:27). At Wendy's lowest point, while she was desperately in need of a hero, she found the only One able to lift her out of her rock bottom, and He set her feet on new ground.

I suppose we shouldn't really be surprised when we see God work the impossible in the lives of hurting people. After all, history proves that to be His specialty—healing the broken, restoring the weary, redeeming the persecuted, and forgiving the worst of sinners. If I would have been alive a couple thousand years ago, I would have liked to hang around Paul. When I read Paul's writings in the New Testament, I imagine a guy who walked humbly, ever mindful of his past and ever grateful for the second chance he found in Christ. He had none of the "holier than thou" attitude that other teachers of the law and Pharisees carried with them. Rather, he was always quick to highlight his lowest lows so that much could be made of the hero who saved him.

> Christ Jesus came into the world to save sinners—of whom I am the worst. But for that very reason I was shown mercy so that in me, the worst of sinners, Christ Jesus might display his immense patience as an example for those who would believe in him and receive eternal life (1 Timothy 1:15-16).

Paul was basically echoing the same sentiment that Wendy did in the last sentence of her story. "If God can save someone like me, anything is possible!" God took a persecutor of Christians and transformed him into one of the most passionate and influential Christ followers in the Bible. God took a pregnant woman in prison and transformed her into a loving single mother with a bachelor's degree and her own home!

Do you need a hero today? Have you ever felt like a lost cause? Perhaps you have reached a point in your story like Wendy did, and you feel just a little too far out of even God's reach. Or maybe you find yourself passing that type of judgment on someone else who has hit their personal rock bottom. I pray that you will come to know the hero in Paul's story. I pray that you will call on the same hero from Wendy's story and invite Him to be the hero in your story as well. Just remember, "Nothing is impossible with God."

He can make a broken heart break into rejoicing.

He can teach a slave to sing a new song of freedom.

He can turn a lost cause into a cause for celebration.

Yes, with God, anything is possible. Now sing it with me: "JESUS, YOU'RE MY SUPERHERO…"

9

THE STORY OF
A BROKEN GIRL

From Amanda...

I'm the little girl who is pretending to sleep,
the covers over my head as I hear him creep.
Into my room he comes over to my bed;
I feel shame and guilt and I am filled with dread.

I believe that Jesus wept as I slept.

At church I hear of a God that loves me,
He comes to save and He is always with me...
How can this be...when you look at me?
I might be cleaned up and dressed in my Sunday best,
but on the inside my heart is broken
with murky waters flowing through my chest.

How can God heal the walking wounded?

I truly am that little girl. I found God's love, and I know He is faithful
to deliver grace for me...for me to forgive the people who abused
me and to forgive myself. Sometimes the enemy puts those pictures back in my head, and the shame of those days surfaces, trying to condemn me...But all I have to do is hand each memory to
God, and I know He will throw it away...I am forgiven.

I am amazed to hear of all the abuse that is going on in this world…
"Those secrets" are happening every day. I am now 47 years old
and am happy in the Lord, and He is the reason I can keep going.
Last week I found out that my 8-year-old niece has been being
molested for the past year and a half by her mother's boyfriend.
Her mom walked in, and thank God, she caught it in "progress."
Her mom called the police, and now we have to wait for justice.

*The LORD is close to the brokenhearted and saves those who are
crushed in spirit* (Psalm 34:18).

Matthew Responds…

Today's devotion is one I wish I did not have to write because this
story is one I wish I never had to read. It deals with such an ugly part
of life and the broken world we live in. But truth be told, out of more
than ten thousand stories that I collected for this project, one in every
five dealt with the topic of sexual abuse. I was shocked, stunned, and
angered as I read story after story from women who had been the vic-
tims of horrible crimes, women whose innocence was stolen away. Sitting in the cabin one afternoon, watching these stories of abuse begin
to pile up before my eyes, I broke down in tears. I thought, "How could
someone do this? How could people dive so far into their sin that they
would steal the innocence of a precious child?"

But here is what really struck me. The vast majority of these stories
were sent to me by people inside the Christian community. I did not
advertise this project in *People* magazine or on MTV. There were no
posters placed in bars or brothels. These women who were carrying the
heavy weight of past abuse had only a few ways to hear about *The Story of
Your Life*—at one of my concerts, on a Christian radio station, or at their
church. These stories were coming from inside the walls of the church.

And yet abuse is a topic that I have rarely heard addressed in today's
churches. I could not help but wonder if that is why many stories of

abuse that I read started like this: "I've never told anybody this before." Many felt as if they had no one to talk to, and perhaps they felt more comfortable anonymously sharing their broken story with a stranger through a letter than risking sharing their story with someone at their church and potentially being met with judgment.

These stories compelled me to dig a little deeper and do some research on this topic. I discovered that one in every three girls and one in every six boys will be molested by age 18. Notice, that's not one in every three girls whose parents don't go to church. No, these stories that lay before me proved that topics such as abuse do not discriminate. This explained why one in every five stories I read dealt with this subject. I also discovered that 88 percent of cases of sexual abuse are never reported.

This means that many of the people living in the world today—walking into a church on Sunday, showing up at your workplace on Monday morning—are hiding the heavy weight of shameful scars from past abuse, and we have no clue. Many walk through their lives, too afraid or ashamed to tell anyone, and as a result, true healing never begins for that chapter of brokenness that was written for them.

If you have never been the victim of abuse, please do not be quick to turn the page. There is a valuable takeaway for you today, and I pray you will not miss it. I encourage you to let Amanda's story and the sobering reality of hurting people in a fallen world sink in for a moment today. Let it open your eyes, just as reading all of those stories opened mine. Maybe even let it break your heart today. Let's not find ourselves beyond the ability to see the world the way Jesus did—through eyes of compassion.

Don't settle for assuming that the people you see in church on Sunday have it all together. Instead, ask God to help you love others as if they might be desperate for someone's kindness. As you do, you may find that God opens up opportunities for you to become that trusted confidant for someone in need of counsel. But unless we see people through eyes of compassion, we will miss the opportunities. Hurting people are all around you every day. Turning a blind eye to this reality results in writing a story with your life that completely misses the point.

Perhaps you have been the victim of some type of abuse. Maybe Amanda's story could very well be a chapter from your own personal story. Maybe you struggle with the same guilt Amanda did, being made to believe that somehow it was your fault. First, I want you to know that the abuse you have suffered is not your fault. You are not to blame. You no longer have to carry that burden of guilt with you. "Come to me, all you who are weary and burdened, and I will give you rest. Take my yoke upon you...for my yoke is easy and my burden is light" (Matthew 11:28-30).

Second, you need to know that you are not alone. As we've seen in today's verse, "The Lord is close to the brokenhearted and saves those who are crushed in spirit."

And finally, restoration is real, and it can take place in your life. But you have to be willing to open up to someone—a counselor, a trusted friend, a spouse, or a mentor at your church. Asking for help is the only real way of receiving it. And help is out there waiting for you to take the first step. The footnote below contains a resource for you to consider as you pray about taking the first steps to restoration if you have not yet done so.*

Perhaps today's devotional has come as a bit of a shock to you, just as Amanda's story did to me. The truth is heartbreaking: Every ten seconds, an innocent child is abused or molested in America—more than three million children a year. What will you do with that information today? Will you gloss over these statistics or let them sink in? Will you turn the page and move on or carry this with you today? Will you choose to stay inside the safe assumption that everyone around you is fine, or will this drive you to your knees to pray for a fallen world where such sin exists? What's it going to be?

---

* www.mercyministries.org

10

HE MAKES ALL THINGS NEW

From Jason...

My mom and dad divorced when i was little. i remember waiting for my dad to pick me up one day, but he didn't show. We moved soon after. When i was 12 or 13, i talked to him for a while, and then he disappeared again. When i got older, i prayed and told myself that if i ever got married and had a boy, i would be the father i never had.

Well, i did get married, and God did bless me with a wonderful boy. I love that boy very much, and my feelings haven't changed about being the best father to him that i can. When i heard you were doing this, i was so excited. i have been wanting to somehow get the word out to boys and even men—to let them know that even though it hurts when someone walks out on you, it wasn't your fault. Not only that, but there is the one and only Father who will never leave you or forsake you.

I hope you can help me get the word out to help all those feeling this way. Thank you for your time and God bless.

Therefore, if anyone is in Christ, the new creation has come: the old has gone, the new is here! All this is from God, who

reconciled us to himself through Christ and gave us the minis-
try of reconciliation (2 Corinthians 5:17-18).

Angela Responds...

Sometimes these are the first words out of our mouths: "It's the way
I grew up." Many of us apply that explanation to a million situations.

"I don't like family get-togethers; it's the way I grew up."

"Hugs make me feel nervous. We didn't do that growing up."

"I don't help my children with their homework because when I was
growing up, my parent's didn't help me."

On and on...The lives we knew as children can explain a lot.

Our childhood can explain our fears, our anxiousness, and even
our poor choices. It can help us understand how our personalities were
shaped and why we have made some of the choices we've made. Some
of us had difficult upbringings, and that explains a lot. Others of us
had fabulous, idyllic childhoods, and because of them, we've got the
good kind of explaining to do.

But some days, it's so easy to let the shortcomings of our childhoods
excuse our decisions as adults. How you and I grew up is an explanation for the feelings we have and the weakness we may face. But at
some point, the man or woman who follows Jesus can no longer use
the explanation as an excuse. Because of Jesus, anyone—anytime, anywhere—can be made new. With God, we do not have to be limited
by the childhoods we had, the earthly fathers who left, the moms who
died too soon, or even the abuses we suffered.

Jesus came, lived, taught, and died so that you and I can have eternal life. But Jesus came for so much more. Through Jesus, we have
received power that can change our very natures. How you grew up
doesn't have to dictate how you will live your future. You do not have
to live in bondage to the struggles you have faced, the people who disappointed you, or the rejection you have known. Our Savior, Jesus, has
made a promise: Anyone who is in Him is a new creation. The old has
gone. The new has come!

That means it's never too late to become anything with God. Your willing heart is the perfect soil for God's new growth in you. Want to be the father you never had? Your heavenly Father has never forsaken you. He will show you how. Want to become the woman you have always dreamed you could be? The power of the Holy Spirit is able transform your heart, your mind, and your spirit. Want to live in obedience when most of your past has been about disobedience? That's just the kind of thing Jesus is able to do. He can take the old away and make you brand-new.

To be in Jesus is to decide to follow His teachings and respond to His leading. We pursue a relationship with Him by reading His Scriptures, praying to Him, and loving and serving as He would have us to. Being in Jesus means that He covers us. His forgiveness covers our past, His power covers today, and His faithfulness covers our future. In Christ, all things are possible. Little boys who had a rough start can become great men. Abused girls whose hearts were broken can become loving moms. This world and its troubles can cause us great heartache, but it cannot have us. We belong to God.

Today, may we look back to our childhoods for explanations that give understanding. But let each one of us come to Jesus and lay our excuses at the cross. We do not have to live as our old selves. Behold, Jesus makes all things, even me and you, brand-new!

Let us live as the new creations of Christ for His glory and for His purpose so that the world can see His goodness and grace.

11

DON'T MISS IT

From Kim...

My dad passed away on January 8, 2005, at the age of 80. He served as a US Marine in World War II and was a gifted musician. But the lifestyle he lived and the choices he made caused much brokenness in my family.

On December 23, 2004, as he lay in the hospital bed, uncertain about his health, life, and future, he asked my mother what he needed to do to ask Jesus Christ into his heart and life. He was at a crossroad with a serious eternal choice ahead. He prayed the sinner's prayer and was transformed into a new creature, as evidenced by his words, actions, attitudes, and heart. I spent one last day with him before he died, and I wrote in my journal throughout the day. I was astonished at the change that took place in him and knew that others would be too.

At one point he looked at me and said, "I missed it, didn't I? I absolutely missed it."

All I could say was, "Well, you're not missing it now. You've got it right now. And now is all that matters, because it is all we have."

Here are a few of his last words, written as a song for his funeral. They reflect the authenticity of a man's heart once he learned the secret to a life that's meant to last forever. I just wish he had found it sooner.

The Miracle in Me

As I lie here in the quiet, thinking back on all the years
The memories, the places, where I can't fight back the tears
They told me I'm a miracle, I had to help them see
Jesus is the miracle, he came alive in me

All I had to do was ask him, ask him to come in
All I had to do was open up my life, my heart to him
It doesn't take intelligence or wealth or looks, just faith
It only takes the asking, for his amazing grace

All along life's journey you find this to be true
Everything has a reason, he put it there for you
We don't always see it, for some it takes much time
It seems to be a struggle we all face in our mind

Amazing grace how sweet the sound
That saved a wretch like me
I once was lost but now I'm found
Was blind but now I see
Now I see the miracle lives in me

I have come that they may have life, and have it to the full
(John 10:10).

Matthew Responds...

"I missed it, didn't I? I absolutely missed it." These were the sobering words spoken from the mouth of a man lying on his deathbed. Vernon was taking inventory of the story he had told with his 80 years, only to arrive at the sad conclusion that he simply missed it. At first read, I was so saddened by Vernon's troubling discovery. Imagine getting to the end of your life, and as you flip back through the pages of your story, you find yourself flooded with regrets. Among the many regrets Vernon had—a failed marriage, broken relationships with his kids, and poor life choices—I sense that he regretted not stopping and taking inventory of his story sooner. Henry David Thoreau wrote, "Most men lead quiet lives of desperation and go to the grave with the song still in them."

I came across a website the other day and noticed this blog headline: "39 Ways to Live and Not Merely Exist." Intrigued, I read further. Some suggestions seemed positive enough to point in the right direction. Number 9 said, "Turn off the TV." Not a bad start. According to A.C. Nielson Co., the average person who lives at least sixty-five years will have spent nine years watching television. Nine years!

Number 37 suggested, "Make an awesome dessert." I suppose this could bring some momentary happiness. Someone once said, "Sleep till you're hungry; eat till you're sleepy." I must say I've lived by that principle a time or two.

Number 6 read, "Follow excitement." Sounds like some good advice, right? I mean, everyone wants to experience the thrill of adventure in his or her life. Adventure is what Edward Cole and Carter Chambers decided to follow during their last days on earth. The movie *The Bucket List* portrays two men from different walks of life who were diagnosed with terminal illnesses and were inconveniently assigned to share a hospital room. In time, they struck up a most unusual friendship, and after weighing options of how to spend their remaining days of life, they decided to come up with a bucket list—a list of things they wanted to do before they "kick the bucket."

With that, they took off on an amazing journey. They climbed to the top of pyramids of Egypt. They rode motorcycles along the Great Wall of China. Dinner in Paris. A safari in Africa. They even went skydiving. But each destination only led them to a search for something deeper. With every item they crossed off their bucket list, they found themselves without peace and seeking something more, something that required more than just time, food, or adventure.

In Carter's final attempt to help his friend Edward find fulfillment before it was too late, he wrote these words in a letter: "My pastor always says our lives are streams flowing into the same river toward whatever heaven lies in the mist beyond the falls. Find the joy in your life, Edward. My dear friend, close your eyes and let the waters take you home."

Jesus offers us more than any best bucket list ever could.

- *He offers us joy.* "I have told you this so that my joy may be in you and that your joy may be complete" (John 15:11).

- *He offers us adventure.* "What no eye has seen, what no ear has heard, and what no human mind has conceived— the things God has prepared for those who love him— these are the things God has revealed to us by his Spirit" (1 Corinthians 2:9-10).

- *He offers us purpose.* "For we are God's handiwork, created in Christ Jesus to do good works, which God prepared in advance for us to do" (Ephesians 2:10).

- *He offers us life.* "I have come that they may have life, and have it to the full" (John 10:10).

"Life to the full." Sounds awesome doesn't it? But what exactly is "life to the full"? Well, I suppose the answer is different for every story. But the only true way to find out what "life to the full" means for you is to make the commitment to unquestioningly follow God anywhere He leads. Talk about adventure! There is no greater adventure than placing your story in the hands of your Creator and vowing to follow His plan into the great unknown. This is the only way to be sure you will not go to your grave with a song still concealed in you or a story untold.

I encourage you to write down Vernon's sad statement on a piece of paper. "I missed it, didn't I? I absolutely missed it." Place it somewhere visible, somewhere you will see it often this week, such as your bathroom mirror or the bottom of your computer screen. Let his words challenge you to take inventory of your story.

And be encouraged by the hope in Vernon's story. See, he didn't miss it altogether. He found the secret before it was too late, and now his story lives on in eternity. It does not matter where you are in your life, whether you are eight or eighty. If you are reading this right now, it's not too late. Life to the full is waiting. Don't miss it.

12

TESTED FAITH

From Kimberly...

This May, my husband and I will celebrate our twentieth anniversary. Before we were married, we aborted a child. Two years ago we both received healing from the abortion and traveled to the National Memorial for the Unborn to have a memorial service for our son, whom God named Aaron James.* After we were married, we had two more children. Both have forms of autism.†

When our son Connor was diagnosed at age two, we were told that only 50 percent of parents of autistic kids stay married because life with autism is so difficult. Connor is now 16, he is preparing to take his driver's license test, and he is studying to be a nurse. He wants to be a nurse so he can help others. Our oldest son, Dylan, was diagnosed at age 9 but is now 18. He is a senior in high school and has been accepted to college for the fall. He will be majoring in national security. His desire is to fight against terrorism.

Our family has struggled emotionally, financially, and in other ways, but one thing that has never changed has been our faith. At times when my faith waned, my husband supported me, and I have done the same for him. My husband and I are very different from

---

* See www.memorialfortheunborn.org.

† For help with autism, see www.autism-society.org and www.autismspeaks.org.

each other, but the Lord knew exactly what He was doing when He put the two of us together.

Dear friends, do not be surprised at the fiery ordeal that has come on you to test you, as though something strange were happening to you. But rejoice inasmuch as you participate in the sufferings of Christ, so that you may be overjoyed when his glory is revealed… So then, those who suffer according to God's will should commit themselves to their faithful Creator and continue to do good (1 Peter 4:12-13, 19).

We boast in the hope of the glory of God. Not only so, but we also glory in our sufferings, because we know that suffering produces perseverance; perseverance, character; and character, hope. And hope does not put us to shame, because God's love has been poured out into our hearts through the Holy Spirit, who has been given to us (Romans 5:2-5).

Angela Responds…

Sometimes when I read the story of people whose faith has been tested, I silently declare to myself, "I don't think I could do that." Maybe you've felt the same way too. I'm sure I feel unable because my attention is focused on the difficulty in their story, the seemingly insurmountable circumstance, the heartbreaking diagnosis, the trials. And I even begin to wonder, "Where does that kind of enduring strength come from? And how does any faith survive so much suffering?"

When we focus on the trials, everything can seem hopeless, but the Bible calls us to another focus. All throughout the Scriptures, we learn about keeping our eyes on the glory of God. The apostles even instruct us to do the very thing it seems no one could do—rejoice. The writers tell us to "rejoice in our sufferings." Maybe the first question to pop into your head is, how? How does anyone rejoice in suffering? In the testing of their faith?

I think we learn to rejoice in our testing because through the testing, we learn what to believe about God.

We learn that our trials are not surprises to God. He has a purpose in everything that has been allowed. And His purpose is always about shaping us into the image of Christ. Teaching us in every trial to look more and more like Jesus. Turning our hearts and minds toward Him.

We learn that Christ is with us. We participate with Him in suffering, and He with us. He has promised to never leave us or forsake us, and He meant it. The testing of our faith brings an intimate knowledge of Christ with us. His compassion toward us. His mercy for us.

We learn that people who are tested by their trials can choose to stay with God or wander away in their anger. When there are no answers, people who are tested have to choose what they believe and whom they will turn to.

We learn that our trials produce in us a character that cannot be shaped by any other means. That we are tested so that we will become people of perseverance, character, and hope. That truly great people have become stronger in their suffering.

We learn that a future joy awaits us in eternity, where there will be no more trials and no more pain. And our hearts eagerly await our promised home in heaven. And it's okay to long for where we were made to be.

We learn that God has given to us the Holy Spirit to be the comforter. That He is able to comfort us in ways we would never have understood apart from the test of the trial. And we learn to receive the comfort only God can give.

We learn that God is faithful to care for us and all that concerns us.

We learn that God gives great hope in the midst of what we never believed we could endure. And the hope of God carries us.

Here is what I find amazing: to encounter people who have known suffering I cannot imagine and then to hear about God's faithful presence to them, His lessons of strength when they were weak, and the blessings they received in the testing of their faith. They are people who have learned to take their eyes off their trials and turn their focus toward God.

May we become people who face the tests of our faith with a determination to rejoice in every suffering. May we become people who believe the purposes and plans of God even when we do not understand. May we who are suffering live every day as testimonies to the glory and faithfulness of God.

Today, in all these things, rejoice.

13

THE VOICE OF THE FATHER

From Kay...

He was charming and funny, handsome and sweet—an absolute dream in any girl's eyes. How was I to know that deep down, darkness was laying in wait? Then something as innocent as a bowl of ice cream sent him into a rage and left me jagged and weak. Did I run? No, with denial high, I married him one fine day in May.

Then the put-downs came, followed by blame, curses, threats, and jealous fire that seared my heart. I cowered under the tables, behind every chair—anywhere I could pretend to hide. Who are you? What am I doing here? When will I see the light of day? Where am I anyway? And why am I living this lie? My heart caved in with each new stab. Eggshells crackled beneath my feet. I wore forgiveness like a badge, and tried, in vain, to leave my fear by the door. And every time the charmer returned, my heart played the same song—the darkness will never come again; the light will shine forever. I knew it was a lie, but there was no place left to hide.

But when he told me I didn't deserve to be forgiven, my soul was set on fire. God *always* forgives me. Who are *you*? The lies came tumbling down. I left without looking back. Now I'm shining in the bright light. I won't forget my darkest night, but I'm living this lie no more.

> *I am the good shepherd, I know my sheep and my sheep know me...My sheep listen to my voice; I know them, and they follow me* (John 10:14,27).

> *"For my thoughts are not your thoughts, neither are your ways my ways," declares the* LORD. *"As the heavens are higher than the earth, so are my ways higher than your ways and my thoughts than your thoughts"* (Isaiah 55:8-9).

> *Dear friends, do not believe every spirit, but test the spirits to see whether they are from God, because many false prophets have gone out into the world* (1 John 4:1).

Angela Responds...

There is evil in this world. Sometimes it comes to us masked behind charm and promises. Sometimes the evil is more blatant and plain—curses, physical blows, threats...However the evil comes, its origin is always Satan. Satan is the father of lies, the whisperer of shame, the accuser of Christ followers. Satan says, "You have to stay no matter how you are treated. You deserve the punishment. You caused everything you've received. No one else would ever want someone like you. You are nothing. You cannot be forgiven. You are ugly to God."

Satan speaks for himself, and his lies come from the pit of his evil. But Satan will never speak for God. And so here is the question: Can you tell the difference between the voice of God, your Father, and the voice of Satan, who is your accuser? When you hear those condemning phrases in your head, do you lean in and listen, as if God were speaking? Do you take the lies of the accuser down into your heart and let them guide your decisions? Does the voice of Satan make you afraid that he's right, afraid that you deserve even worse than you have received?

Listen, my friend. God does not contradict Himself. He cannot be other than He is, and He is always the same—yesterday, today, and tomorrow. He is not wishy-washy with His love. He loves you with an everlasting love that can never change. He does not take His forgiveness back. If you have asked, He has forgiven, and it is done for all eternity. God does not play games with your heart; neither is He the author of confusion or fear.

Do you know how to tell the difference between the voice of evil and the voice of God? The evil accuser will always remind you of your sin. He will keep bringing it up until you are paralyzed with guilt and shame. He will make you doubt the complete forgiveness of God. He will make you suspicious of God's love. He will twist passages from the Bible and use them for his own misdirection. He wants you to live spiritually uncertain, hesitant, mistrusting, and insecure.

But oh, hallelujah, there is One who is holy and good. The voice of our God is faithful to His Word. When He speaks to you, He will never contradict His own Scriptures. He will not bring confusion to you. Instead, the voice of God gives wisdom. The voice of God is our Father's voice, calling you toward His forgiveness, His healing, His restoration.

Maybe you are only beginning to learn the voice of your Father. Sheep know their shepherd's voice because they have spent time with the shepherd. The same is true for us. We will know our Father's voice because we have been with Him. We desire to know Him. We long to hear.

Today, if evil speaks to you or shouts to you or calmly entices you, I pray you will recognize the source. I pray you will not be fooled by the voice of the accuser, but will reject every lie he offers. May your words and your choices demonstrate this response: "Satan, I will have no part of your lies. Your power over me has come to an end."

Even more, I pray you will be quick to hear and respond to the voice of God. You are His beloved. He is your Father, your Redeemer, your Protector and Friend. His love for you is everlasting.

14

EVERYONE HAS A STORY

From Kristin...

My life story? Ordinary. Simple.

From Melissa...

I don't have a very dramatic story. I just love God.

> *When Jesus looked up and saw a great crowd coming toward him, he said to Philip, "Where shall we buy bread for these people to eat?" He asked this only to test him, for he already had in mind what he was going to do.*
>
> *Philip answered him, "It would take more than half a year's wages to buy enough bread for each one to have a bite!"*
>
> *Another of his disciples, Andrew, Simon Peter's brother, spoke up, "Here is a boy with five small barley loaves and two small fish"* (John 6:5-9).

Matthew Responds...

We never find out much about him. His name was never mentioned. He was simply referred to as "a boy." "Here is a boy with five small barley loaves and two small fish." He had anything but a starring role in John's account of the day Jesus fed 5000 people. Supporting cast at best. And after Jesus performs this incredible miracle, we never hear about the boy again. He was nothing but a tiny little footnote in an epic story of a miracle-working Savior.

Easily forgotten? Yes. Easily replaced? Not so fast. Think about it. There were 5000 people following Jesus that day, and they were starting to get hungry. So Jesus sends His disciples out into the crowd to see what kind of food they can scrounge up—and this is the best they can do? All they found was "a boy" with nowhere near enough food to feed all the people who were waiting. And this boy could have easily held back what he had. He could have kept it for himself. He could have said, "Hey, it's not my fault I was the only one who thought to pack a lunch." But instead, he gave all he had—five small loaves and two small fish.

This tiny little act of obedience became the spark Jesus used to light a fire in the hearts of thousands as a miracle of multiplication took place before their very eyes. "A boy" became a hero. Oh, not the kind of hero who took home the headlines. He was never given his own book of the Bible or anything like that. He wasn't the star of the story. But he was in the right place at the right time with the right response.

I have a feeling the boy's role in the story was no surprise to Jesus. John says in verse 6 that Jesus already had in mind what He was going to do. Jesus knew He was about to do the incredible. He also knew that boy had a valuable role in this miracle story. All the boy had to do was faithfully step forward, offering up what he had. Score one for the common folk! What an awesome example of God's choice in heroes! If someone told me I could have one sentence (and only one sentence) written about my life in the Bible, I would want it to read like this boy's did. He simply obeyed. The right time, right place, right response.

I love the movie *Simon Birch*. Simon was a peculiar boy to say the least. He was extremely short (due to a rare birth defect) with big, Coke-bottle glasses and a scratchy voice. When looking up the word *common* in the dictionary, one would not be overly surprised to see a picture of this little boy. Yet throughout the movie, Simon holds firm to the belief that God made him the way He did for a reason, constantly referring to himself as "God's instrument." During one scene, he discusses his purpose with the reverend at his church.

> SIMON: Does God have a plan for us?
>
> REVEREND RUSSELL: I like to think He does.
>
> SIMON: Me too. I think God made me the way I am for a reason.
>
> REVEREND RUSSELL: Well, I'm glad that…uh, that your faith…uh, helps you deal with your…um, you know… your…your condition.
>
> SIMON: That's not what I mean. I think I'm God's instrument—that He's gonna use me to carry out His plan…I want to know that there's a reason for things. I used to be certain, but now I'm not so sure. I want you to tell me that God has a plan for me, a plan for all of us. Please.
>
> REVEREND RUSSELL (struggling to come up with a good answer): Simon…I can't.

Perhaps you too have wanted to believe that God has a plan for you, that you are His instrument. Maybe like Simon, you've been told it isn't true. Have you heard voices of doubt that have caused you to question whether God really does have anything special in store for you? Do you feel as if your story is boring or ordinary? Or that you don't even have a story at all?

Remember today that your existence here on earth is proof of your purpose. You would not be here if not uniquely designed and planned by the Creator of every living thing. Consider these Scriptures as powerful reminders that…

- *God made you.* "Before I formed you in the womb I knew you, before you were born I set you apart; I appointed you as a prophet to the nations" (Jeremiah 1:5).

- *God knows you.* "For those God foreknew he also predestined" (Romans 8:29).

- *God chose you.* "For he chose us in him before the creation of the world to be holy and blameless in his sight" (Ephesians 1:3).

The trouble is, when searching for the purpose of our story, we often set our sights on some glorious and far-off horizon, assuming that if God is going to use us, He must have something big in mind. And while we are busy looking off in the distance for our moment to shine, we miss the everyday "loaves and fishes" opportunities to be God's instruments. Some of the greatest heroes in God's kingdom are not those with special talents, dramatic testimonies, or positions of power. No, like the boy with the loaves and fishes, they are the faithful, the obedient, the ones who are committed to serve the Lord in everyday, ordinary ways, being mindful all the while that at any moment, God could carry out one of His miracles through them. I am convinced the streets of heaven will be filled with such heroes—the ones who never received any name recognition on earth. Why? Because their ambition in life was to lift up the name of a miracle-working God.

Heroes like Dawn. Dawn and I grew up in church together. Dawn was always on fire for God. Her passion for Christ was contagious. One Sunday, she and three others in the church were about to be baptized, and my dad asked each of them to share their story. I was in the front row. I always loved baptism Sundays, and I sat on the edge of my seat in the front row as I listened to exciting stories of people's lives being transformed. This particular Sunday did not disappoint. We heard stories of addiction and stories of depression. Fascinating stories of people who had been rescued by God from the edge of despair.

Then it was Dawn's turn. The others had taken us on adventures, leaving the church breathless by the drastic twists and turns their stories had taken. Dawn, only a high school student at the time, took the microphone, and in a quiet, somewhat apologetic voice said, "Wow. Well, I…uh, I don't have much of a story compared to everyone else. I just love Jesus and want the whole world to know."

I will never forget what my dad said as he stood up to address the congregation and she handed him the microphone. He looked at her and said, "Dawn, you have the most exciting testimony anyone could ever have to tell because it is uniquely yours. You love Jesus with all of your heart, and He is going to use you in a mighty way." He was right. Today, Dawn and her husband are church planters reaching the lost in the inner city of Boston. They're not concerned about name recognition; they're just making sure the name of the Lord is known everywhere they go.

Isak Dinesen said, "To be a person is to have a story to tell." Maybe you grew up in a Christian home and never fell off the deep end. Maybe you don't have a dramatic story of conversion, but like Dawn, you "just love Jesus and want the whole world to know." Don't be discouraged by that. Be encouraged by the promise that you are God's instrument. And step forward into the rest of your story, knowing that those who waste less time worrying about name recognition and invest more time making His name known are the real heroes of heaven. And you are well on your way.

15

FORGIVEN

From Sarah...

My story is one of forgiveness...I fit the profile of the typical Christian girl who grew up in the church. It wasn't until high school that I started going down the wrong path. I got involved with the wrong guy and ended up losing my innocence to him. Not too much later, I found out I was pregnant.

I made the decision to have an abortion on my own—I didn't tell my mom, my sisters...anyone. I couldn't bear the shame of admitting my failures. Years down the road, after counseling, I am able to look back and realize that even though I turned my back on God for quite a while during that experience, He was standing right next to me all the time, holding His hand out for me to grab hold. He forgave me the second I confessed and asked Him; I just had to forgive myself.

It's incredible to experience His blessings years down the road. I am newly married to a wonderful Christian man, and God continues to rain down blessings. I know He has a plan in all this, and I am ready and willing to go where He leads.

The Lord is compassionate and gracious, slow to anger, abounding in love. He will not always accuse, nor will he harbor his anger forever; he does not treat us as our sins deserve or repay us according to our iniquities. For as high as the heavens are above the earth, so great is his love for those who fear him; as far as the east is from the west, so far has he removed our transgressions from us. As a father has compassion on his children, so the LORD *has compassion on those who fear him; for he knows how we are formed, he remembers that we are dust* (Psalm 103:8-14).

Whoever conceals their sins does not prosper, but the one who confesses and renounces them finds mercy (Proverbs 28:13).

Angela Responds...

Everyone. Christ died for everyone. For every sin, for every awful thing we've ever done that seemed like the only choice at the time. There are no exceptions with Jesus. No sin is too terrible to be forgiven. No distance is too great for Him to reach across. There is no one whom our Savior considers unforgivable.

Jesus offers the gifts of forgiveness, salvation, and eternal life to everyone. The last verses of the Bible give one final appeal to anyone who needs God: "Let the one who is thirsty come; and let the one who wishes take the free gift of the water of life" (Revelation 22:17).

The forgiveness and salvation Jesus offers are gifts. They cannot be earned or achieved. You cannot be good enough to attain the forgiveness Jesus gives. We come to Jesus empty-handed, with nothing to offer. We are forgiven because of Christ's sacrifice and compassion for us. We would not be able to earn forgiveness even if we tried. Forgiveness is freely given to any who ask.

But like any gift, the gift of forgiveness is not yours until you choose to receive it. I can buy a gift for my daughter, wrap it beautifully, and tell her about it. I can even put the gift into her hands. But until she unwraps the gift and takes it as her possession, she does not have what I wanted to give to her. She might even put the beautifully wrapped box on a shelf and look at it for years, never knowing what glorious gift was hidden inside.

So many of us have done the same with the truths of God. The Bible that sits on a shelf contains the truths of God's great and merciful gifts to us. But those gifts will not belong to you until you choose to receive what Jesus longs to give to you.

It's so easy to decide, "I don't deserve forgiveness. My sin is too great. I've waited too long. I am not worthy of Jesus compassion." But in case you missed it somewhere, that's kind of the point with God. None of us deserve the forgiveness He offers. To receive a gift you could never deserve—that's called grace. Christ died on a cross (what we deserved) so you and I could be forgiven of our sins (what we didn't deserve). God desires that we receive His gift, unwrap it, and make its truth our possession. He wants us to live forgiven lives so others can know about His goodness and His grace.

It is not God's heart that you live every day of your life punishing yourself for your sin. No matter what you have done—abortion, adultery, burglary, extortion—there is no sin beyond the reach of grace. The Bible says to all of us, "There is now no condemnation for those who are in Christ Jesus" (Romans 8:1).

To be forgiven means the condemnation is over. Jesus paid the punishment you deserved, and He forever ended any need for condemnation. There is absolutely no limit to the forgiving, life-changing, merciful grace of God.

Maybe one of the most powerful things we can do as the forgiven is to give what has been given to us. When you have been forgiven much, you want everyone to know what you have received. What if we who have been forgiven freely granted forgiveness to others as quickly as God gave it to us? What if we turned toward forgiven sinners with "no condemnation"?

How amazing it is to stand before God now that we are forgiven. How beautiful it is to take others to the giver of forgiveness and watch Him make their lives clean. May it be so in your life and mine.

16

YOUR FAMILY TREE

From Rebecca...

When I was a child, my home was filled with homosexuality, mental illness, anger, and violence. The legacy my parents were leaving me was sure to lead to a life filled with emotional turmoil.

But then came Jesus. I found Christ at a young age, and He walked beside me all the days of that difficult childhood. It didn't mean everything was better or easier, but I was never alone. And most importantly, He gave me a new legacy.

One of the most poignant moments in my life came when I was an adult and my father was dying from AIDS. I was standing in his home, talking with his partner, while my mother and father were in the adjacent room angrily arguing about emotional battles and suicide attempts. I had a sick feeling in my stomach as I listened to a conversation that embodied the very sad reality of all I had known as a child.

My father's partner responded to what we were hearing by saying to me, "Well, I guess that's your legacy."

I responded with a resigned, "Yeah, I guess so." But the moment that I uttered those words, God spoke to my heart with unmatched depth and clarity when He said to me, "*No*, this is not your legacy. You have My legacy because you are My child." That truth has made all the difference and always will—for eternity.

One thing I do: Forgetting what is behind and straining toward what is ahead, I press on toward the goal (Philippians 3:14).

Matthew Responds...

My grandmother was an incredible woman. Luella West gave birth to ten children! Now, that's just plain crazy. She had nine boys and one girl! Now, that's *really* crazy. With a family that big, you know it's a pretty safe bet that there were some broken branches in my family tree. Every family has its doses of dysfunction, and I guess my family was no exception. My grandpa was a hardworking man, but my dad tells me that back in the day, Grandpa liked to drink a little. Well, actually, he drank a lot. And Grandma was pretty fed up with it.

One night, Grandpa came home drunk, and Grandma decided she was going to teach him a lesson. She marched into the kitchen and grabbed the biggest cast-iron frying pan she could find. Then she marched back to Grandpa West and smacked him upside the head with it. Now, let me state for the record that I do not condone or encourage this type of action, but I must also say that I can't deny the result. See, after Grandpa came to, he never took another drink of alcohol! My dad told me it served as a real wakeup call in his life. (I'm sure it would wake me up too!)

Soon after, Grandpa started taking the whole family to church, and he accepted Christ into his heart. He was a changed man. And that's not all. One of the kids he brought to church was my dad. My dad found God when he was 17, and he has been a minister now for more than 35 years. My parents gave birth to me, and now I'm writing this devotional you are reading. And to think, all it took was one person making a choice (with a little encouragement from a frying pan) to change his direction in life. That choice has influenced generations of our family tree for the better. We joke now that some follow the 12-step program, but Grandpa followed Grandma West's one-step program!

Truth is, many people in the world are struggling through their lives, believing they are destined to drag along the heavy generational baggage that was handed down to them. Somewhere along the line, they have believed the lie that they are bound to re-create the dysfunction that has defined their family trees. Maybe you have heard lies like these and been tempted to believe them:

"You're gonna be an alcoholic, just like your daddy was."

"Your marriage is just going to end in divorce, just like your parents' did."

"Depression runs in your family. Get used to it."

"You come from a long line of losers. You're just another link in the chain."

These lies have one common, demonic goal: to prevent anyone in your family tree from finding new life. Rebecca was tempted to believe those lies. She was so defeated by her dysfunctional surroundings, she was ready to give in and just believe that since she came from dysfunction, she was bound to recreate dysfunction. But truth spoke up. And with a resounding *NO!* Rebecca was flooded by the promise that she has received a new legacy.

My Grandpa and Rebecca both demonstrate that all it takes to start a new legacy is one person. All it takes is one to drop the generational baggage once and for all and take hold of the truth that no one need be defined by yesterday. "One thing I do: Forgetting what is behind and straining toward what is ahead, I press on."

God has a plan to use you to breathe new life into your family tree. The chain can be broken, the bags can be dropped, and a new legacy can begin. Let it begin with you.

17

TURN ANOTHER PAGE: JOY COMES IN THE MORNING

From Kaela...

Five hours from home, I sit in a tiny college dorm room and wonder—what's the use of going on? Why even bother trying to live in this world? I spent the last week starving myself and listening to these doubts in my head, making me question why I even exist.

> *He reached down from on high and took hold of me; he drew me out of deep waters* (Psalm 18:16).

> *Weeping may stay for the night, but rejoicing comes in the morning* (Psalm 30:5).

Matthew Responds...

The classic holiday film *It's a Wonderful Life* begins with a conversation in heaven between God, Joseph, and a second-class angel named Clarence Oddbody. Clarence has yet to earn his wings and has been called upon to help a man named George Bailey, who is facing a world of trouble. George's financial crisis has led him to such despair that he is standing on a bridge, staring down at the icy waters below, and contemplating taking his own life. So Joseph sends for Clarence, and God speaks to this eager angel: "A man down on earth needs your help."

Clarence responds, "Oh, splendid! Is he sick?"

God answers, "No, worse—he's discouraged."

More than 20 million Americans are dealing with the serious illness of depression, many asking the same question Kaela asked: "What's the use of going on?" I met a mother in California who, with tears in her eyes, showed me a picture of her 28-year-old son who jumped off the Golden Gate Bridge, taking his own life. This young man came to a place in his story where he just couldn't bear the thought of turning one more page, and a life story tragically ended way too soon.

What brings a person to such despair, such hopelessness? Maybe you know the answer to that question. Maybe you're battling such discouragement today. Or maybe as you are reading this book of stories, you notice just how many have dealt with pain or brokenness or trials. So much heaviness and sadness. Perhaps you are thinking, "Where is the joy?"

The world sees way too many Christians living stories void of victory, with the glaring absence of joy. Matter of fact, if the world is looking at me on any given day, they very well may fail to see any joy either. I'm the type of person who can have 99 out of 100 things going perfectly well, but guess what I'm thinking about? Yep, that one (often small) little piece of the puzzle that isn't fitting exactly the way that I want it to. All too often, I let the little things steal my joy. I'll give you a humbling example.

Not long ago, my family and I packed up and headed to the beach for a family vacation. We rented a little house that I assumed would be right next to the water. I could just imagine waking up each morning to the sounds of the ocean coming through my bedroom window, soaking up the salty air from my back deck while enjoying my morning coffee. However, we arrived to find our beach house was actually across the street from the beach, a whole three blocks away. I know, right? How dare they!

Well, I wish I could say I just rolled with it, choosing to be happy and just thankful to be anywhere near the beach. But truth be told, I let that one tiny little detail bother me so much that I was unable to enjoy the beach the whole first day our vacation. (I eventually snapped out of it.)

See, even the little frustrations or discouragements of life can threaten to rob us of our joy. But God promises over and over again in Scripture that our stories can be filled with a joy that will radiate throughout our entire lives.

All we have to do is ask: "Ask and you will receive, and your *joy* will be complete" (John 16:24).

All we have to do is spend time with God: "You will fill me with joy in your presence" (Psalm 16:11).

All we have to do is turn the page: "Weeping may stay for the night, but rejoicing comes in the morning" (Psalm 30:5).

The Reverend Billy Graham once said, "The Christian life is not a constant high. I have my moments of deep discouragement. I have to go to God in prayer with tears in my eyes and say...'Help me.'" Even Billy Graham, a man of great faith who has preached to millions of people around the world and counseled every president since Dwight D. Eisenhower, recognizes the reality of debilitating discouragement. Satan knows that a Christian's joy on display is a dangerous thing because it is contagious. When people see the joy of the Lord alive in us, they will want to know where it came from and how to get this same joy in their lives. This is why the evil one will stop at nothing to try to discourage you today.

Are you stuck at a point in your story where, like Kaela, you are wondering why you should even turn another page? Well, regardless of how far down you find yourself, cling to this promise today: "He reached down and took hold of me...he drew me out of deep waters" (Psalm 18:16). Your deep waters of discouragement are no match for the joy unspeakable that you have been promised today. I challenge you to memorize these powerful reminders that we can be rescued by joy so that when darkness or depression comes, you may be armed with the truth that outshines the lies.

You can cry out to God with the same simple prayer Billy Graham prayed—"Help me"—and He will. He really will.

Your heavenly Father is alive and living in you. So turn another page, knowing that joy comes in the morning.

18

OUTLIVE YOUR LIFE

From Susan...

People always commented how Will was such a special person and how they believed he would grow up to be in the ministry in some capacity. Will too felt that calling, but things were interrupted at the age of 16 when he was diagnosed with leukemia. He reached remission that same year but relapsed at the age of 17. He was sent to Duke Medical Center but never reached remission again. When the doctors told him there was little hope of regaining remission, Will made the decision to stop treatments and spend his remaining days with his family, away from doctors and hospitals. His remaining six weeks would stun us all.

He preached several sermons and recorded several popular Christian songs. But one of the most amazing things that has come out of his illness is the vision God gave him to start a ministry to reach out to young people. Checklist Ministries was Will's vision, and while at Duke he told his dad exactly what he wanted to do and how he wanted to do it. Since Will's death, his dad, along with help from others, has made this ministry a reality, and it will host its first event this Saturday in Union, South Carolina at Will's home church. Six hundred to seven hundred youth are expected to attend.

People continue to come to us and tell us how Will changed them forever with his unbelievable faith and courage during such difficult circumstances as fighting leukemia. In the end, even knowing death was certain, he never gave up on God. Will was a true man of God during his 18 years of life. God had a purpose and a plan for him, and it played out perfectly. And although we are still hurting from losing him, we know that awesome things have happened as a result of his illness and death, and we know that we will rejoice with him in heaven one day.

My goal is that they may be encouraged in heart and united in love, so that they may have the full riches of complete understanding, in order that they may know the mystery of God, namely, Christ, in whom are hidden all the treasures of wisdom and knowledge (Colossians 2:2-3).

Angela Responds...

What if God never intended the length of your life to be the most important thing about it? What if all along, God has wanted us to understand that what really matters is the way we fulfill the purpose of our lives, regardless of the number of days we have been given?

There is only one way to live with purpose, and that is to live your life according to the truths of Scripture. That includes knowing who you are because of Jesus and what He has done for you, as well as deciding to pursue what He has called you to do on this earth. Maybe coming to understand your true identity as a Christ follower is the most beautiful characteristic of a life well lived. Do you know what it means to belong to Christ? It means...

- Your sins are forgiven so you don't have to walk around in shame and guilt anymore. You are free to live in the joy of your forgiveness. And you are free to give to others what you have been given.

- Your home in heaven is safe and sure, so you don't have to worry about the future.

- You have been given the indwelling presence of the Holy Spirit, who will lead and direct your life if you will stay close to Him. You don't have to have all the answers or figure everything out by yourself.

- Your life has purpose, regardless of how unfocused you feel or how lost you have been. God has always had a plan for every day He has given to you.

To live every day in God's will means following Jesus today. That's all. One day at a time, living in relationship with Jesus Christ. Not getting ahead of where God wants you to be today. Listening. Depending. Obeying.

When men and women live each day dependent on Jesus, His purpose for them is clearly revealed. The Bible teaches that our overarching purpose is to know Christ and to use our unique gifts to make Him known. But the details come in our daily, step-by-step walk with Christ, asking each day, "What does Jesus want me to do today? Where is He directing me to go? What does He want me to give? Where can I obey? Serve? Build? Grow?"

For most of us, learning to live Jesus-dependent means that we very deliberately make Christ our first priority and our focus. Without intentionally choosing to do this, we human beings just wake up focused on ourselves—on our fears and our wants. Being human is our natural inclination, but following Jesus first is a choice we make from day to day, hour to hour, and encounter to encounter. To live your God-ordained purpose means living as Jesus leads. None of us can hear His voice from a distance. We must choose a relationship with Him to be close enough to follow.

And so today, will you stop worrying about where the time is going or when you will get it all done? Will you decide that what matters is how you will walk with Jesus in these 24 hours? Will you go where He leads? Speak as He guides? Love as He loves? Will you choose Jesus today in all that concerns you?

To live a life with great purpose is not some big, grand goal that hardly anyone ever attains. To live with great purpose usually means faithfully taking small steps in the direction of Jesus every day. Whether you have six weeks or sixty years left on this earth, you will outlive your life when your day-by-day obedience builds a legacy that brings glory to God long after you are gone.

19

LETTERS FROM RUTH

From Ruth...

About three years ago, I was sitting in my car and waiting for my kids to come out of school, when a boy walked in front of my car. As soon as I saw him, I felt the Lord tell me, "Pray for him."

I didn't know who this boy was, I didn't know his name, I didn't know his story...but I did know that God wanted me to pray for him. I remember telling the Lord, "I don't even know him. What do I pray about?"

And I felt his response was, "It's not for you to know yet. Just pray." So I did, for two years. Later, I found out this boy's name was Jake, and he had been in trouble a lot. I knew in my heart, though, that this boy was going to do great things for the Lord one day. I could feel it when I prayed. I knew that he would change the lives of those around him.

Well, one night (about a year ago), I was watching the evening news. Suddenly I saw Jake's mug shot on the television screen. He had been involved in a serious crime and was going to spend time in jail. Needless to say, my heart sank. But all I could think was, "Does Jake know that Jesus loves him? Is anybody in that jail telling him?"

Then I felt Jesus tell me, "You tell him."

So I said, "Okay, Lord, I will." I wrote Jake a letter and told him that Jesus loved him regardless of what he had done or where he had been. I thought that would be the only letter I sent Jake, but Jesus had a different plan. Over the next six months, I would write Jake 75 letters. Each letter was about the love of Christ, about His forgiveness and grace. I wrote about my personal struggles and experiences, and I taught him about the Bible and about the people in it. I even taught him how to read the Bible.

All this time, Jake never even knew who I was. I had never talked to him face-to-face. It took a while before I included a return address because I didn't really even want a response from him. I just wanted to tell him what Jesus needed him to hear.

Well, one day I received a letter in the mail from Jake. I cried as I read it. He told me that when he was first in jail, he lost all hope. He didn't think he could ever be forgiven by his family, his church, or even God. But when he received my first letter and read the words, "Jesus loves you…" his outlook on everything instantly changed. Hope returned, and he knew he could make it through his time in jail and his life would change for the better. He knew God had put him in jail for a reason and he would stay there as long as God needed him to, even if it meant going to prison. Then he told me that he had accepted Jesus into his heart while he was in there! Praise God!

Six months later, Jake got out. Amazingly, we ran into each other at Applebee's. He came over to the booth I was sitting at with my son, and he hugged me and thanked me for writing him and telling him all about Jesus. And get this (this is just so amazing to me)— he told me that a lot of the guys in that section of the jail (about 40 men) read all of the letters I wrote him. They would ask him every day, "Did you get a letter from Ruth today?" And then they would pass it around. Some of them even wrote down all the Scriptures I included in the letters. Isn't that just like Jesus! He was working in ways that I never even knew. Praise His name!

Now Jake is out and doing well, and he often comes over for dinner with my family. He is truly a testimony of the greatness of God! "Did I not tell you that if you believe, you will see the glory of God?" Jake and I believed…and we have seen the glory of God.

This is how we know that we love the children of God: by loving God and carrying out his commands. In fact, this is love for God: to keep his commands (1 John 5:2-3).

Give me understanding, so that I may keep your law and obey it with all my heart. Direct me in the path of your commands, for there I find delight (Psalm 119:34-35).

Matthew Responds…

Every Tuesday morning, my wife, Emily, volunteers at a local women's shelter called Mercy Ministries that we support in Nashville. One morning as Emily was preparing to head to the shelter, my daughter Lulu ran to her as she opened the door to leave, wrapped her arms around her mommy's leg, and asked, "Why do you have to go, Mommy?"

Emily answered, "Well, honey, I am going to help some people and tell them about Jesus." Lulu thought about it for a second (still completely wrapped around my wife's leg) and then responded, "Can't someone else do it?"

My actions sometimes seem to echo the same response to God. "Can't someone else do it?" Sadly, I have often felt a prompting to reach out to people and share the love of Christ with them in one way or another, only to back out and choose not to act. My reasons always seem so rational in the moment. "Oh, I'm sure that person doesn't want to be bothered." "The homeless shelter probably has more volunteers than they even know what to do with." Each time I rationalize my way out of God's invitation to share His love, am I actually saying, "Can't someone else do it?" And does that grieve His heart?

On the other hand, there are times in my life when I have responded the way Ruth did when she felt God calling her to reach out to Jake, a troubled teen in jail. (I hope that as I grow in my journey of faith, these times will become more and more frequent!) Her response? "Okay, Lord, I will." And look at the result! After reading Ruth's first letter, "hope returned" in Jake's life, and God's love washed over him. What's more, several other prisoners found encouragement through those letters.

What if Ruth had never written that letter? What if her response had been, "Can't someone else do it?" Perhaps someone else would have reached out to Jake—we will never know. But we do know that God used Ruth's letters in this young man's life, and they helped to bring him to a powerful turning point. In addition, Ruth witnessed firsthand that amazing things can happen when we simply step out in obedience and say, "Okay, Lord, I will." Our obedience is the key that opens wide the door of God's blessing both in our lives and the lives of those we obediently reach out to.

Find encouragement today in God's track record of rewarding those who are obedient to His call on their lives.

- Daniel was obedient, and God kept him safe in a den of lions (Daniel 6).
- Joshua was obedient, and God gave the Israelites the city of Jericho, just as He had promised (Joshua 6).
- The disciples were obedient, and God reached the first Christians through their ministry with Jesus (Matthew 4:18-20).

You see, we cannot even begin to imagine how God might use our simple acts of obedience to reach hurting hearts in need. Ruth began writing letters, and a young man's life was changed. Remember Ruth's story today, and when you feel God calling you to step out in obedience, don't assume someone else can do the job. God is calling *you*. Every day God gives you chances to impact the story of someone's life for eternity. All you have to say is, "Okay, Lord, I will."

20

WATCH ME

From Luanne...

"Watch me."

How many times have I been told, "You're not gonna make it" or "You can't do that"?

And how many times have I replied, "Watch me"?

Sometime ago, when I was a missionary in Haiti, a few visiting missionaries asked me to take them to the citadel. The citadel is a huge fortress built on the top of a mountain by Haiti's first king, Henry Christophe. As we began the climb up the mountain, we saw several men with bony horses offering rides up the mountain. My first thought was that riding up would be a lot easier that walking, but I was with energetic young people who wanted to walk, so I decided to walk with them.

As we were climbing the mountain, one man with a horse kept saying "Man, you ain't gonna make it." At times I wasn't so sure he was wrong. My body was saying, "He's right, you know—you're not gonna make it." My heart was pounding out of my chest, my legs felt like jelly, and my lungs were about to burst.

But my personality has a stubborn streak. When people tell me I won't be able to do something, they light a spark in me to prove them wrong. So I kept my eyes on the top of the mountain and kept telling myself, "You can do it. If others have done it, so can you."

I've since realized that the Bible is full of people who wouldn't give up.

When people told Noah, "You'll never finish that boat," Noah replied, "Watch me."

When Sarah laughed at the thought of God granting her a baby, God said, "Watch me."

When the Egyptians thought Moses could not lead the Israelites out of their dead end, Moses said, "Watch me."

When the people of Jericho said Joshua could not enter the city, Joshua said, "Watch me."

When Goliath laughed at the thought that a shepherd boy could defeat him, David said, "Watch me."

When Jesus' disciples thought Jesus couldn't provide enough food for an entire crowd, Jesus replied, "Watch me."

When Martha said Jesus was too late to heal Lazarus, Jesus said, "Watch me."

When Satan accused mankind and said, "They're not worth saving," God said, "Watch me."

I was reminded that day of the many times in my life when someone said to me, "You're not gonna make it."

I graduated with my high school class when I was eight months pregnant. My mom didn't think I would hang in and do it. I said, "Watch me."

When I was 20 years old and lying in an intensive-care bed, the people who loved me were worried that I wasn't going to make it. I never thought I wouldn't.

When I talked about going to nursing school, someone I admired laughed. I thought, "You just watch me."

Only during my divorce did I think I wouldn't make it, but God said, "Watch me."

When I decided to become a missionary, the evil one told me, "Never! You're divorced, you're a nobody...who would want you?" I turned to my Lord, and together we said, "Watch me."

As I neared the top of that mountain in Haiti, I clung to God's promises that in Him all things are possible, and I said, "Watch me."

I can do all this through him who gives me strength (Philippians 4:13).

I look to you, heaven-dwelling God, look up to you for help. Like servants, alert to their master's commands, like a maiden attending her lady, we're watching and waiting, holding our breath, awaiting your word of mercy (Psalm 123:1-2 MSG).

Angela Responds...

Some people seem to think they have been assigned the ministry of discouragement. I run into them all the time, and I bet you do too. Even more sad, I've been the recipient of their attempts and jabs. They are the naysayers. The pessimistic and gloomy. The cowardly. They are the "It's too big and you're too little" kind of people.

The discouragers are a motley group who can take you by surprise. Sometimes an adversary will try to dishearten you, but more often it's the person who loves you who gives the stinging blow. The one you turned to for support. The friend you hoped would cheer you on. Their words squeak out, the discouragement sinks in, and the weight of their disapproval presses your spirit down.

And then the undoing begins. Discouragement makes you doubt what you've started. You wonder if the discouragers are right. Maybe somebody like you shouldn't attempt something so big after all. Your confidence takes a hit.

Here is what I love about God. Right there, right in the middle of your doubt, even as you're rubbing the wound you've received...that is where the Holy Spirit rushes in to renew you. The Bible says that every-thing God has called you to do, He will give you the strength to do. Regardless of what anybody says, if God has called you, His strength in you will make it so. And when the Holy Spirit inside of you restores your courage, you can continue to follow God and whisper, "In the name of Jesus, watch me."

But there are days when more than new courage is needed. The battle weary have nothing left. The wounds are too many. The top of the mountain is too far. God has known since before we were born that you and I could not save ourselves. But oh, praise God, we have a Sav-ior. We have a Deliverer, a Rescuer, and a Friend. We have One who is able when we are undone. One who forgives, heals, restores, and redeems. Jesus, the Son of God, is our Savior.

> When the hopeless call on His name,
> when the desperate cry out for His mercy,
> when the lost weep tears in their abandon,
> the God of heaven shouts across creation, "Watch me."

21

THE GOD WHO SEES

From Kelli...

I was a single mom raising a 16-year-old son and a 10-year-old daughter. My son was a junior in high school, and he decided he wanted to join the West Virginia Army National Guard. In 1996 the country wasn't at war. He was adamant, he knew I couldn't afford college, and he was convinced that the National Guard would take care of all his college expenses. None of his other friends were enlisting. This was what he wanted to do. He had always been a wonderful son, easy to raise, never any difficulties. He was about to turn 17 and was able to enlist with his parent's signature.

I didn't know what to do. I was left to make the decision on my own as his father wasn't in the picture. I struggled for some time and prayed about it constantly.

Every night my 10-year-old daughter wanted me to read her stories from a children's Bible we had. One night we came to the story of Hagar in the desert, with Hagar determined she would die there. Hagar was the first single parent mentioned in the Bible. God appeared to her and reminded her of the promises He had made and told her that His promises were still true.

All of a sudden I stopped reading, tears came to my eyes, and I wanted to shout "Thank You, Jesus!" That was my answer. God was with my son and had always provided for us! I knew my answer. I signed the papers, and my son went off to basic training at age 17. He left me in West Virginia and went to Missouri during the summer between his junior and senior years of high school. That was hard on a mom.

He did fine, came back, finished his senior year of high school, and entered college after graduation. He was right—the National Guard supported him well in college. During his last semester of college he was deployed to Iraq. "Wow, Lord, are You sure?" After ten months in a foreign country, he returned home and finished college. He married later that year, had two small children, and now, six years later, he is being deployed to Afghanistan.

I constantly have to take myself back to that desert and remind myself of God's promises to me and my son. He has taken good care of him and his family. My son is employed full-time by the National Guard and is currently a first lieutenant with hopes of being promoted to captain. The Lord has kept many of His promises to me, but I will never forget the evening when He gave me that answer and reminded me of the promises He had already kept.

The angel of the LORD found Hagar near a spring in the desert; it was the spring that is beside the road to Shur. And he said, "Hagar, slave of Sarai, where have you come from, and where are you going?"

"I'm running away from my mistress Sarai," she answered.

Then the angel of the LORD told her, "Go back to your mistress and submit to her." The angel added, "I will increase your descendants so much that they will be too numerous to count"...

She gave this name to the LORD who spoke to her: "You are the God who sees me" (Genesis 16:7-10,13).

Angela Responds...

Hagar's circumstances had become awful and confusing. Her ability to change anything seemed hopeless. So Hagar did what a lot of us think about doing when life is really tough. She ran away.

Have you ever wanted to run away? I sure have. Several years ago, when I was a single mom raising four kids, I decided I had two runaway plans. Plan A was to run away to Montana. For some reason, I was sure people in Montana would be nice. And when people in your life are mean, you just want to go where everyone is nice. I was going to move there with my kids and get a job as a café waitress, and the hardest thing I would have to do is ask, "You want fries with that?"

Plan B was more serious. I considered it when I thought I would die if I had to live through one more difficult and irrational encounter. Plan B was to sell everything, buy homeschool books, and move with my kids to Africa. There we would live in a hut and raise corn. Truly, I always thought we would grow corn. And if I was frustrated with the children, I told them they would have to run around naked through the corn stalks in Africa.

Hagar was a plan B kind of person. Extreme pain called for extreme measures. Hagar ran away into the desert to die, and a person does that only if she believes with every fiber of her being that she has no hope. In her mind, anything and anywhere—even death in a desert—would be better than what she was leaving. Hagar believed she was all alone in this world. She had no one to care for her or her unborn child.

Then there was Genesis 16:7, and the angel of the Lord, who just happened to be God Himself, found her. God spoke to Hagar, and she realized she was not alone. God saw her and cared for her. He gave her direction ("Go back to your mistress and submit to her") and a promise ("Your descendants...will be too numerous to count").

Hagar gave God the Hebrew name *El Roi*, which means, "the God who sees." Can you imagine her overwhelming joy right there in the middle of that desert? "He sees me! God really, truly sees me!" Hagar gave God a new name and renamed the well nearby, but most importantly, Hagar obeyed God. She went home, and God kept His promises.

I love that Kelli knows what it means to be seen by God. He saw her enduring the pain of letting her son go, and He gave her comfort and peace from the story of Hagar. This very day, God sees Kelli and her heroic son in Afghanistan, and He sees you. No one is invisible to God.

Maybe this can give you comfort today: The God who sees you is the same God who keeps every promise He has made.

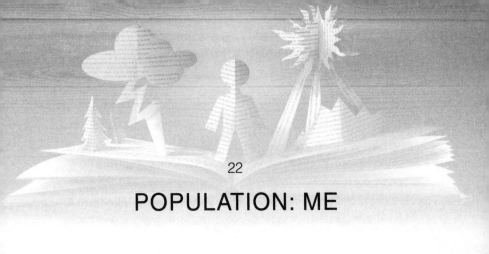

22

POPULATION: ME

From Joy...

"When I grow up I want to be a missionary." These were my words at the age of seven. Twelve years and four overseas mission trips later, that dream has not changed. My heart is with the poor. I cannot look at pictures of orphans, or see the elderly sitting on the side of the road, without seeing the pain, joy, fear, and most of all, hope in their eyes. I long to know and impact their stories. While I live a life of comfort, going about my daily college routine in the states, I ache to be among the needy. I can't wait to see how God will use this passion to take me places in the future! I want to spend my whole life reaching a lost and hurting world, bringing hope and purpose to their stories.

From Jessica...

I came from the pits of such a dirty place in my life. When you experience things like I have, your eyes change. You see differently. It is not so important to go tanning or get your nails done. You begin to look around, and a passion is created. My heart is for the homeless man holding the "Will work for food" sign in the Walmart parking lot. I hurt for the children in Haiti who are parentless and hungry tonight. The world is so overwhelming, it would be easier to keep my eyes closed. But I know God has a purpose for me to help those people who are in need.

From Michelle...

When I was in the hospital, a nurse took care of me and showed me love, patience, and compassion through my uncertain, terrifying illness. And as my life went on, I realized that the people I met there made a difference in my life in a positive way. They have all led me to Jesus and to His unselfish caring and love for us. Through that nurse's kindness, I was led to become a nurse as well and give back.

Here I am. Send me! (Isaiah 6:8).

Defend the weak and the fatherless; uphold the cause of the poor and the oppressed (Psalm 82:3).

Whatever you did for one of the least of these...you did for me (Matthew 25:40).

Matthew Responds...

The other day, I read a tweet update by Rick Warren that said, "To make an impact with your life, answer three questions: What needs to be done? Why not me? Why not now?" So I decided to retweet the message. (For those who are not hip to the Twitter lingo, that means to forward someone else's message on to the people who follow you. Very confusing, I know.) I followed his questions with a few of my own from my song "My Own Little World."

What if there's a bigger picture?
What if I'm missing out?
What if there's a greater purpose
That I could be living right now
Outside my own little world?*

One woman's response to my messages made me laugh out loud (or LOL, in Twitter talk). In response to all of the challenging questions I was posing, she responded, "Geez. I'm just trying to figure out what to make for dinner! Challenge me tomorrow?"

I must say, I appreciated the honesty of her response. Do you ever feel like that? You know there is a bigger picture. You sit in church and hear the pastor talk about all the needs in your community. You turn on CNN and learn of earthquakes that leave thousands homeless. You know the world needs you. Meanwhile, you're just trying to keep your own world afloat and your head above water. Regrettably, this is my situation on most days. But recently, my life was changed and my eyes were opened to see how different the world can look when we shift our perspective.

I spent two months in a cabin reading 10,000 stories. Stories came in from all walks of life and all parts of the world. The stories featured in this book were all read in the cabin. For two months, I focused on the stories of other people's lives. For two months, my perspective shifted from me to them. This experience absolutely rocked my world, and God used these stories to reshape my purpose in life.

There was a pivotal moment one day in the cabin when I felt God reveal a convicting truth to me. This is what I wrote in my prayer journal: "Spending two months focusing on the lives of other people has made me humbly aware of how differently I live the rest of my life. Most days go by, and I don't even spend two *minutes* focusing on anyone other than me. I'm tired of 'population: me.'"

At the risk of sounding overdramatic, I could feel my heart being transformed in that cabin. I found myself crying with those whose stories were touched by tragedy, rejoicing with those who told me about the great miracles they had seen God do in their lives, and challenged by the tremendous need for hope in our world. It was as if God were saying, "See, this is how the world looks when you lift your eyes off your own circumstances. This is how I see the world. I am calling you to join the bigger story. The world is bigger than you. Only when you realize this will the story of your life reach its greatest impact. As long as your life is all about you, I cannot use you fully."

And this is the great irony of our quest for purpose and meaning in life. We plan for our retirement. We invest in our 401(k)s and purchase four-door sedans. We take care of ourselves and our families. We cheer for our football teams. And then we sit back and wonder why we still feel unfulfilled. Mack Douglas wrote, "Dedicate yourself to a cause greater than yourself, and your life will become a glorious romance and adventure." Jesus wants to lead us into that adventure.

We are called beyond just a one-dimensional story. We are called to a story line that runs deeper than our own. Diane Ackerman writes, "I don't want to get to the end of my life and find that I lived just the length of it. I want to have lived the width of it as well." Don't you want to live the width of your life too? There is only one real way to do this— by making a choice to see beyond your own little world.

Dr. Robert Pierce is the founder of World Vision, one of the largest world relief organizations in the world. They are daily in the business of carrying out the message of the gospel by caring for the orphans, the poverty stricken, and the sick. Dr. Pierce's prayer is one that I have begun to pray myself: "Let my heart be broken by the things that break the heart of God." This is where the adventure begins. Once you open your heart to a cause greater than yourself, you begin to write a story with your life that will leave a greater legacy than any 401(k) ever could. Scary? Yes. Risky? At times. Worth it? Absolutely. Consider Rob Brezsny's challenge:

> This may be the turning point your grandchildren will tell stories about years from now: the time you leap over the abyss to the other side of the Great Divide and begin your life in earnest. On the other hand, this moment of truth may end up being nothing more than a brief awakening when you glimpse what's possible on the other side of the Great Divide, but then tell yourself, "Nah, that's waaayyy too far to jump." In that case, your grandchildren will have to be content talking about what delicious cookies you used to bake or what your favorite sports team was. It will all depend on how brave you'll be.

I pray that today's devotion may serve as a moment of truth for you. Will you dare to step outside your own little world? Will you enter in to the adventure you were made for? Jesus is calling you to reach the world outside your door. Will you be brave enough to answer, "Here I am. Send me!"

23

RESTORED

From Laura...

In 2001, my husband and I were divorced. We had been married 13 years and have four beautiful children. I still had many issues from childhood abuse to deal with, but in the next four years or so, I felt God was healing me in many ways. However, in mid 2005, I reacted to verbal abuse from my boss and walked out on a very good job.

This led to a year and a half of being in the wilderness. I lost absolutely everything tangible—all my friends from work and eventually my home. My family became dependent upon God for food, shelter...everything. I had once worked more than 70 hours a week, but I now found myself with an enormous amount of time on my hands and no one but God to fill it. God placed me in His Word, and I did study after study.

During this time, I learned that God is the true healer and that there is a huge difference between believing in God and believing God and His promises. When we lost our home, we moved to a small duplex, where I slept on the couch and gave the kids the two bedrooms. Yet we knew we were in God's hands, and we were filled with joy.

God later restored me and gave me a great job. Shortly thereafter, He healed my broken marriage and gave back the years the locust had eaten! My husband and our four children were reconciled, and he and I have been remarried for more than two years. God truly does turn bad into good when we seek Him with all our heart! He healed me in areas I didn't even realize still needed to be healed, and I can truly say just as Job did, "My ears had heard of you but now my eyes have seen you." More importantly, I learned there is *always* hope in God. Nothing is impossible for Him! And though His ways are certainly not our ways, His ways are always best!

I will repay you for the years the locusts have eaten... Then you will know... that I am the LORD your God, and that there is no other (Joel 2:25,27).

Then Job replied to the LORD: "I know that you can do all things; no plan of yours can be thwarted... My ears had heard of you but now my eyes have seen you" (Job 42:2,5).

Angela Responds...

Yesterday I found my son's iPod between two cushions in the sofa. When I returned it to him, all his music listening enjoyment was instantly restored. Maybe if I found a purse on the street, I could return it to the owner and restore her financial security. But to restore the life of an entire family? Return to them the love, joy, and peace they once knew? Give more blessing than they had ever imagined? Only God can do something like that.

restoration |, res-tə-'rā-shən|

noun

1 the action of returning something to a former owner, place, or condition

Restoration is such a beautiful theme with God. We see it in the book of Job, in the locust-ridden history of the Israelites, and in the stories of our own lives. The plotline begins with a familiar scenario: complete and total brokenness. Lost people searching for answers. Hopelessness giving way to despair. Then one day, the defeated turn their cries toward God—His faithfulness, His love, and His power. And all throughout history, in His time and in His way and at His will, God restores.

Maybe you just read Laura's story and thought to yourself, "That's great for her. She has a beautifully restored life, but nothing like that could ever happen for me." Do you know that the same God who restored Laura and her family longs to show His faithfulness to you? He does. The God of glory is at work all around you. Your circumstances are not unknown to Him. He is not sleeping through your heartache. He has not misplaced His plan for your future. Laura told us her story because she has lived years of brokenness, negative consequences, and pain. She wants us to know that if God is big enough and merciful enough to restore her, He can and will do the same for us.

But there also seems to be a theme for the restored. Broken people turn their lives toward God, and not just for a day or a few prayers. These desperate people fall across His altar and stay there, believing Him to be their only hope.

Are you willing to turn and give every broken thing to God? Broken people keep waiting, as if they finally understand that God moves in His time, according to His purposes, and always for His glory.

Will you wait for the God who restores? His restoration of broken people is always more than they could have dreamed. Marriages are renewed. Wayward children come home. Addictions are broken. New dreams are given.

Do you trust God for more than you ask, imagine, or hope for? Oh, my friend, I pray that Laura's story is just the thing your broken heart needed to hear. I pray that her wait and her heart for God will inspire you to trust in the God of healing. Bring your pain, bring your embarrassment, bring your mistakes...bring them all to Him. And then, will you wait? What if you wait for seven years, as Laura did? Or ten, or even more? Wouldn't it be something to see God restore to you all the years the locusts have eaten?

And here's one thing I have learned about God: When He restores what has been taken from you, He gives back multiplied! God loves to show off His glory, doing what no one ever believed could be possible.

May all of us who are broken come and wait for God. I pray for a day very soon when you will look at His restoration in your life and declare with the people of God through the ages, "My ears had heard of you but now my eyes have seen you!"

24

OUR OBJECTS
OF DISTINCTION

From Charlie...

I was raised in a family where the motive of life was the superficial intention of building fame and reputation. I followed this model naively and helplessly until I was about 30, when I realized at the top of my game that I was empty. I left it all and from a spiritually dry place screamed out to a God I never knew. He came and got me, gifted me with a Holy Spirit-filled wife, and then brought me back to the career I left; but this time I have a new sense of self and, I pray to God, the pure intention of love backing it up.

In thinking about my life over the years, it always felt like a tale of two mountains, one built of dust and one built of stone. I was standing on the one built of dust. And when I finally realized it and saw the person I wanted to be standing on top of the other mountain, I closed my eyes, tumbled down to the bottom, and began climbing the better mountain. I'm not there yet, but I'm trying, and I'm desperately clinging to the faith and hope that God is pulling me up.

Do not store up for yourselves treasures on earth, where moths and vermin destroy, and where thieves break in and steal. But store up for yourselves treasures in heaven, where moths and vermin do not destroy, and where thieves do not break in and steal. For where your treasure is, there your heart will be also (Matthew 6:19-21).

This is how God showed his love among us: He sent his one and only Son into the world that we might live through him. This is love: not that we loved God, but that he loved us and sent his Son as an atoning sacrifice for our sins (1 John 4:9-10).

Matthew Responds...

Today I was walking through a shopping mall (something I try not to make a habit of) when a storefront window display caught my eye. This was an expensive clothing store that specialized in fine clothing. In the window display, there were tailored suits that cost more than a mortgage payment, Italian leather shoes that looked too nice to walk outside with, and cashmere sweaters looking too expensive to touch, much less wear. This was a store for serious shoppers with serious amounts of money. And that is precisely why I have never entered this particular establishment.

But as I passed by the store, I noticed some words in the display window. I saw one statement, printed in a very elegant font, of course, and it read, "Objects of Distinction." I stopped and read it again, noticing those expensive items beckoning in the background. "Objects of Distinction." The word *distinction* means "a distinguishing or treating with special honor, or favor." Another definition reads, "marked superiority." This store was attempting to get shoppers to buy in to the notion that these expensive items of clothing would, in fact, set them apart and make them superior to others.

Today's devotional is not about the evils of wearing nice clothing. Far from it. I am not saying that having nice things is wrong. But Jesus does warn us in Matthew about the dangers of these so-called objects of distinction. The problem is that all too often, they quietly become our objects of affection. This is what Jesus was talking about when He said, "Where your treasure is, there your heart will be also." And when your heart belongs to nice clothes or any other material treasure, the story of your life becomes a sad tale of misguided affection.

Charlie's story was headed down that path of misguided affection, and he said that path led him to "a mountain of dust." As a result, while he was still at the top of his game, at the height of his success, he realized his life was missing something. And so he made the bold choice to walk away from it all in search of a more meaningful life.

What are your objects of distinction? Do you own something or do something that you feel sets you apart from the crowd? Or maybe you have something in your sights—a particular dream or goal that you are pursuing right now, such as a job promotion or a love interest. Do you ever find yourself thinking, "If I just had that, I'd be set"?

In your search for distinction today, look no further than the cross. Wish you had something that set you apart? Consider this: "You were bought at a price" (1 Corinthians 7:23). The Creator of the world has pursued your heart, even to death on a cross. His love for you is unmatched. His plan for you is unchanging. And His grace for you is unending. You are *His* object of affection.

There is no greater distinction in this life than to be called a child of God. Sure, God blesses all of our lives in different ways. We may be blessed with the clothes we wear or the houses we live in or the jobs we have. But if our love for the blessings in our lives becomes greater than our love for the provider of those blessings, we are sorely missing the point. Be careful not to let your affection be stolen by a lesser object of distinction.

As you walk through your life this week, remember Charlie's choice to pursue the better mountain. Take a good, hard look at where your story is leading and know that what sets you apart from the world is the promise that you are Christ's object of affection and that there is no greater object of distinction than that.

25

ONE LESS

From Greg...

My wife and I started the adoption process of a little girl named Lily from Guatemala in August of 2007. After two and a half years, we were able to finally bring her home in 2009. I am the senior pastor of a church in Tennessee, and our whole family of faith embraced the adoption process.

As a part of the adoption, my wife moved into an apartment in Guatemala so we could foster our now eight-year-old daughter. We spent seven months apart from each other. It was the most difficult test we have faced as a couple, but the pain that marked those seven months was quickly replaced when we finally made it home. The joy we shared when we arrived here reminded me of what it must be like when one of God's children finally makes it home. We left Guatemala with no fanfare and a few tears. We arrived at our home with church members lining the street with banners, cheering, and sharing in our great relief.

Religion that God our Father accepts as pure and faultless is this: to look after orphans and widows in their distress (James 1:27).

Whoever welcomes one of these little children in my name welcomes me (Mark 9:37).

Matthew Responds...

My friends Clark and Angie have a heart for adoption. They have adopted two children, one with Down syndrome. As a result, their time, energy, and finances are frequently stretched to the limit. Still, their desire to care for orphans remains strong, and they are now pursuing a little girl from Russia who has special needs.

I recently asked Clark, "Why do you do it?"

This was his response: "I just have a hard time believing that when I stand before God someday, He would ask me why I gave so many orphans a home." I was speechless. And challenged.

There are an estimated 143 million orphans in the world. To see that each one of them is cared for in our lifetime may be impossible. The best way to begin? One at a time. That is exactly what Greg and Sheila did by adopting Lily. They were about to become empty nesters, with two sons already on their way to college. Sheila told me they had begun saving up money to take their dream vacation to Hawaii. They were right on the verge of taking a stroll down Easy Street, with nothing but comfortable golden years ahead, when a church missions trip to Guatemala changed their hearts and their direction.

Instead of taking that dream vacation, they used the money to embark on a much different journey. They heard of a little girl in the Guatemalan orphanage where they had visited, and after much prayer, they decided that they were the ones to adopt Lily. They still haven't been to Hawaii, but when I saw the way they looked at their little girl, I could tell Hawaii didn't matter as much to them as it used to.

What an incredible story of obedience! The Bible is crystal clear when it comes to orphans and our role in caring for them. "Look after orphans and widows in their distress."

Greg and Sheila chose not to ignore that Scripture. Instead of just assuming that verse was for someone else to carry out, they took it upon themselves to forgo the comfortable path and instead pursue one of obedient faith that led them to a precious little child who now has a mom and dad to call her own.

Wes Stafford is president of Compassion International, a ministry on the front lines in the effort to care for kids in need around the world.

He has been quoted as saying, "I spend half of my life comforting the afflicted and the other half afflicting the comfortable." Perhaps today's devotional will make you a little uncomfortable as well. It is never easy to come face-to-face with the reality of the great need in our world. It is even more difficult to ask yourself, "Am I too comfortable?" But today, I encourage you to ask yourself just that. Then, ask God to show you a way you can be involved in carrying out this vital mission of helping to care for children who are orphans.

Not everyone is called to adopt a child. Adoption is just one of the ways you can be involved in caring for orphans. Many families open their homes to become foster parents. And beyond that, organizations like Compassion International and World Vision provide the option of sponsoring a child from another part of the world who is in great need.*

I received many stories from individuals and families whose lives have been enriched because they reached beyond their comfort to care for orphans in one or more of these ways. They describe in great detail the joy they have found in bringing a smile to a needy child's face.

The chapters from the story of your life that will echo for eternity are the pages that tell of the times you cared for others. Today, ask God to show you how the pages of your story can tell of such servanthood. You will discover joy unspeakable when you know that because you cared, there is one less broken heart in the world.

---

* See www.compassion.com and www.worldvision.org.

26

TWO CHOICES

From Phil...

My wife, Tammy, and I were foster parents for nine years before we had the opportunity to adopt our son, Jamie. Shortly after his adoption in 2007, we took a trip from our home in Maine to introduce him to extended family. In North Carolina, we were involved in a terrible accident that took the life of my wife, uncle, and cousin. Jamie, two aunts, and I were seriously injured. I spent a year in rehab. I also had to return to North Carolina to testify in a trial (the other driver is in prison now).

Through this experience, I have changed my career. I had been a nursing-home administrator, but now I am a minister of music, and I am participating in a parachurch ministry related to foster and adoptive care, long-term care, and the Christian response to grief. God has taught me so much about forgiveness, purpose in life, peace, trust, His sovereignty, and how to think about these things in circumstances that we don't understand.

I have submitted a formal request to meet the other driver in prison. I've been witnessing to this young woman by mail, but I had a vision of myself baptizing her. God can redeem any circumstance for His glory—even the tragedy of losing family members.

Shortly before our accident, Jamie accepted Jesus Christ as his Savior. He asked Tammy several times, "Do I have to forgive my grandfather?" (The grandfather is now serving a prison sentence for abusing our son.)

Tammy replied, "I know it's very hard, but eventually, yes, you'll need to forgive him. Your only choices are forgiveness or bitterness, and I don't want to see you grow up to be a bitter young man. You should pray that God will give you a forgiving heart and that He'll send someone into your grandfather's life to introduce him to Jesus."

Jamie didn't like this answer. Three weeks after the accident, Jamie was my roommate in rehab. I received a letter from the other driver, asking for forgiveness. Jamie told me, "You know, Dad, you're going to have to forgive her eventually. Your only choices are forgiveness and bitterness. You should ask God to give you a forgiving heart and to send someone into her life to introduce her to Jesus." What a wise child! Tammy had only a short time with her son, but what a valuable legacy she left him—the willingness to forgive those who have wronged us in the most extreme circumstances.

Of course, I had to forgive the driver. I was hearing my wife's words telling me to do so, and I had to set the example for my son.

Though you have made me see troubles, many and bitter, you will restore my life again; from the depths of the earth you will again bring me up (Psalm 71:20).

Get rid of all bitterness, rage and anger, brawling and slander, along with every form of malice (Ephesians 4:31).

See to it that no one falls short of the grace of God and that no bitter root grows up to cause trouble and defile many (Hebrews 12:15).

Angela Responds...

Any one of us could read Phil's story and quietly whisper to ourselves, "After all he's been through, he has every right to become bitter. I would be. If anybody is entitled to be angry and hurt and resentful, it's this guy. No one should have to lose so much. His story and loss was unnecessary and unfair."

My heart breaks over Phil's tragic and multiplied loss. Reading his story has moved me to tears. I cry for his family, but oh, my goodness, I also weep over his strength. His powerful, inspiring decision to choose forgiveness instead of bitterness models the kind of strength I want for myself.

Phil's wife said there are two choices, and she was right. One will empty your soul and the other will bring you back to life.

Where are you today? You may not have lost someone you love, but your heart can hold on to bitterness for a hundred different reasons. Just before I began to write, I noticed some bitterness in me today. I felt misunderstood by one of my children, and a seed of bitterness started germinating in me. I knew I couldn't write this devotional until I dealt with this little root that wanted to grow. So I left my computer and went upstairs to my child's bedroom. I lay on the bed and prayed, "O God, take my bitterness and fill me with forgiveness. I choose life. I will not indulge the temptation to keep being hurt over childish things and childish ways. Make me like You. I want to give what You have given to me. Amen and amen."

Bitterness separates us from God. We become deaf to His call to forgiveness and ignore His instruction to get rid of every form of anger. And based on my experience this morning, I should add this: Get rid of it quickly because bitterness seems to grow so fast!

Bitterness also isolates us from other people. When we are bitter, we are painful to be with and our sour hearts make us difficult to love. People tend to avoid us when we are full of bitterness and rage.

When you choose forgiveness, you consciously trust God for His justice. He is the only One who can make things right for you and untangle the circumstances that cause you pain. To choose forgiveness is to return to joy—to enjoy the good that you have been given and to look forward to the good promises of God.

Never underestimate the power of forgiveness because the freedom works both ways. Both the giver and the receiver are set free. To give forgiveness is to gratefully acknowledge what you have lavishly received from God, and to humbly give to others what God has mercifully given to you.

Today, right now, you have two choices.

27

OUR SECRET CHAPTERS

From Steve...

My story is one of guilt, shame, and God's redeeming love and forgiveness.

I was a successful radio announcer for 38 years. I had a loving wife, a beautiful daughter, and a career on the rise. The stress load I carried was immense, and over time I began falling into unhealthy habits. I got involved in looking at pornography on our computer at home, which led me to seeking out an inappropriate relationship with a young woman. I worked early mornings, and as I traveled to work, I stopped and left letters in this woman's car. She consequently left me items as well, thus triggering a desire to return there.

Long story short, I was caught and sent to prison for two years. No one had known of my secret addiction, but now it was headline news. My wife, daughter, and extended family were devastated. I was so ashamed. But getting caught was the best thing that could have happened to me. I was confined in my cell, utterly alone and ashamed. Sobbing in pain, I poured out my heart to God, and I felt a warm peace come over me. It was as if He were sitting beside me, catching my fall with His strong, forgiving, loving hands. It was as if He whispered, "I've got you...you are in the grip of My grace now."

Prison is not a fun place, yet He protected me. As a matter of fact, not long after that, I began singing in the chapel praise band on Sundays. A lot of people surrender to jailhouse religion, claiming to know God when they are incarcerated. But God whispered to me that night that I would take Him with me when I left. And praise God, I have. I wrote these lyrics that night after God whispered to me in prison.

In the grip of your grace I am sheltered
Your harvest of hope leads me on
In the grip of your grace I'm free
In the grip of your grace sin has no power over me
In the grip of your grace is where I want to be
In the grip of your grace

Create in me a pure heart, O God, and renew a steadfast spirit within me (Psalm 51:10).

I the LORD search the heart and examine the mind, to reward each person according to their conduct, according to what their deeds deserve (Jeremiah 17:10).

But among you there must not be even a hint of sexual immorality, or of any kind of impurity (Ephesians 5:3).

Matthew Responds...

I have a songwriter friend who is involved in prison ministry. One day, I asked him what it was like being inside the walls of a prison, speaking and singing for a crowd of convicted criminals. I was curious to know how he was able to connect with them.

He told me, "The first thing I always say when I stand up in front of those inmates is, 'Fellas, I want to make one thing clear. The only difference between you and me is you got caught and I didn't!'" He told me the inmates always erupt in laughter, amused by a free man's candid confession of guilt.

One of the most widely known confessions of guilt was delivered in a hymn that was written in the 1700s.

> Amazing grace, how sweet the sound
> That saved a wretch like me
> I once was lost but now I'm found
> Was blind but now I see

These words could not have been penned by a perfect man. Far from it. John Newton was a slave trader, a cruel and ruthless business-man who made a living selling human lives as slave labor. He experi-enced a dramatic conversion, though, while trying to steer his slave ship through a terrible storm. Believing that God had spared him at sea, he submitted his life to Christ. He later stopped slave trading alto-gether and became a minister, joining William Wilberforce in the fight to abolish slavery.

"…That saved a wretch like me." Webster's defines a wretch as a per-son with despicable character. Judging by Newton's choice of words, it is clear that he was both painfully aware of his sin and eternally grate-ful for his salvation. So is Steve, a man whose sin has led him to places he never thought he would go and caused him to hurt people he never thought he would hurt. Caught in the middle of his own dark personal storm, Steve realized he had nowhere left to hide. His secret sins were secret no more. They had become headline news. I was struck by the story he sent to me.

Steve didn't waste time by trying to build a case for his defense. Not once did he point a finger or attempt to blame anyone else. Steve has come to a place in the story of his life where his secret chapter has been exposed, and all he has to offer now is his own humble confession of guilt and testimony of grace.

Notice how Steve chose to describe being caught and sent to jail. He called it "the best thing that could have happened." Come again? At first read, one would wonder if that was a typo. Yet with his secrets laid bare for all to see, Steve no longer had to carry the weight of his secret chapters. Trying to maintain a Christian image while carrying a secret dark side will wear you down, and eventually it becomes impossible.

I know of a preacher whose church discovered he was struggling with pornography. He had managed to keep his secret chapter hidden for quite some time, but then he returned home from a minister's conference, and the board members discovered charges to his hotel room for pornographic movies. One would think he would have been smarter than that if he were truly trying to keep his secret. However, he later confessed he was trying to get caught so he could finally be free of this secret sin, which was dragging him down.

The thing is, while we are busy exerting so much effort to cover our secret chapters, there is One who sees every part of our stories. "You have set our iniquities before you, our secret sins in the light of your presence" (Psalm 90:8). Nothing is hidden from God. "Would not God have discovered it, since he knows the secrets of the heart?" (Psalm 44:21). H. Jackson Browne wrote, "Character is who we are when we think no one is looking." So who are you when you think no one is looking?

The devil will try to make us believe we can keep our secret sins under control and no one will ever have to know. Truth is, those secret sins control *us*. It is essential to our spiritual survival that we ask some difficult questions and be honest with ourselves about our weaknesses. I have seen way too many men fall victim to sexual temptation, whether through online pornography or extramarital affairs. Their secret chapters have destroyed marriages and ruined lives. To think I am above or beyond such temptation would be nothing short of foolish. I realize that I too must take an active role in creating an environment that helps me avoid temptation, both at home and during my travels. Here are four practical and effective ways I have been able to stay pure.

1. When traveling, I never have my own hotel room. I choose to share a room with my road manager or one of my bandmates. Alone time in a hotel room can be a dangerous thing. It can become way too easy to flip the channels on the television to some movie I know I shouldn't watch.

2. When I am home, I have a few close friends whom I consider to be my accountability partners. These friends are unafraid to ask me the tough questions. I feel comfortable confiding in them and really opening up to them about my struggles.

3. I downloaded a program from www.xxxchurch.com that monitors all of my online activity, flagging any questionable websites that I may visit. It also automatically sends a report to my accountability partners every week, letting them know about my online whereabouts. The key here is accountability. When our secret chapters tempt us to isolate ourselves from others, we must fight back and surround ourselves with people we trust who will hold us accountable.

4. There is a great book called *Every Man's Battle* by Stephen Arterburn and Fred Stoeker, which tackles this difficult and rarely discussed struggle among men. This is a must read for every man trying to pursue a pure, godly life.

Perhaps Steven's story scared you. Maybe you can relate to his secret sin, and you worry that you really don't have it under control after all. Do you feel as if you are being dragged further and further down? Is the balancing act of keeping up a Christian image while hiding your secret chapters wearing you out? You don't have to live like that. Your sins are no surprise to your Savior. When you stand before Him at the end of your life, He will not say, "Oh, I didn't see that part." So stop hiding. Be courageous. Step into the light of grace and allow God to transform your secret chapters into testimonies of redemption.

If you or someone you know needs help with any type of sexual addiction and have no one to talk to, please call 1-800-NEW-LIFE (1-800-639-5433) and begin walking the path to freedom today.

28

THE SUN WILL SHINE

From Alice...

It was pitch black and pouring rain while I drove my two boys away from the nightmare we had been in. Afraid of what my husband would do when he found us missing, I called to tell him we had left. He begged me to stop, to tell him where I was so he could get us. I didn't—I dialed my parents instead. I drove through the tears and the rain, following my dad's simple instructions: Drive here and then call; drive there and then call again. I had only a vague awareness of where we were, but he talked me the rest of the way to a shelter.

The people there led us to a small room. The boys sat on the floor and played while I answered questions and filled out forms. The rules were strict: a set curfew, a set bedtime, the children could not be left unattended, daily chores, no visitors. We were shown our room. It had one single bed and a bunk bed.

We woke in the morning and went for a walk. From the first step outside the door, I knew God had brought us home.

The other day I came across the admissions folder for the shelter we went to that first night. Inside was the picture that my oldest son had drawn while waiting for me to register. On that dark, sad, raining night, he had drawn a picture of a bright, sunshiny day.

You, LORD, are my lamp; the LORD turns my darkness into light
(2 Samuel 22:29).

*Even in darkness light dawns for the upright, for those who
are gracious and compassionate and righteous* (Psalm 112:4).

*He lifted me out of the slimy pit, out of the mud and mire; he
set my feet on a rock and gave me a firm place to stand. He put
a new song in my mouth, a hymn of praise to our God. Many
will see and fear the LORD and put their trust in him* (Psalm
40:2-3).

Angela Responds...

A bright, sunshiny day. That's what God can do with your darkness
too. He can take you by the hand or drive you through the pouring
rain or lift the dark veil that covers your eyes. Our God turns darkness
into light. He brings the dawn of a new day for every dark night. He
lifts up the weak and sets their feet on a rock.

Maybe someone you love lives in the darkness of abuse or some
other sin that has pushed away all the light.* The Bible calls that kind of
life a slimy pit of mud and mire. But our God can rescue us in any situation. No circumstance is too dark, no life us too ugly, and no obsta-
cle is too imposing for Him.

I love that the very first morning at the shelter, Alice knew that
God was the One who brought her and the two boys home. I also love
that her son probably didn't have the words to express what was in his
heart, but his drawing expressed everything he believed. The sun was
shining for them. God drove that family through the night right to
the tiny place He had prepared for them. It was His shelter for His
beloved, complete with rules and chores and simple beds. There, He
clearly spoke to them: "You are safe now. You are loved. You are home."

Maybe your world has been covered in darkness for oh-so long now,
but you've just read Alice's story, you've seen what God did for her, and
your heart has begun to pound a message to your head. You want to go

---

* For help with abusive situations, see www.whatsgoodaboutanger.com/domestic.asp.

home. You want to follow God and trust Him with the journey. You want to go to the place He has appointed for you. Maybe the place will have rules and chores. Maybe the next steps will be like driving through the pouring rain with only one instruction at a time. But it's home... you know God is calling you home. You long for the day when the sun will shine for you.

The light you crave comes only from God. He is the One who gives a new life to people in the slimy pit. He is the One who cleans up the muddy. He carries the weak to the firm place, where they can stand. Do you need to ask God to take you home? Oh, friend, seek Him. Pray to Him. Open a Bible and learn more of Him. He promises a new dawn for the upright. He promises to hear the prayers of the earnest. And this I know of God: If you seek Him with all of your heart, you will find Him. He will find you.

And so for all of us with dark places in our lives, may today be the day we ask God to be the lamp and bring His light to every dark place.

For all who've been away, it's time to go home, into the bright, sun-shiny day of His love.

29

FAITH IN THE MYSTERY

From Nancy...

As all stories do, my story begins and ends with God. Two years after my God-fearing, God-loving husband and I were married, we welcomed our first son. A few years later, after much praying for a daughter, we discovered God's sense of humor when He gave us two more boys—twins.

But then we discovered that our twins have a genetic chronic illness—cystic fibrosis. We learned how to care for them and felt optimistic about their futures. We adopted a baby girl who also has cystic fibrosis. We raised our children to love the Lord, and they grew into amazing adults who are full of imagination. As they left the nest and established their own homes, we felt led to open our home and hearts to foster children. Recently we adopted another little girl, who blesses us daily.

But then life stopped. Our oldest son suddenly died; his wife was pregnant. We looked to the Lord for comfort. We have struggled to understand how God could take away this loving man who was so looking forward to being a dad. We have been heartbroken and confused as we have helped our daughter-in-law raise our sweet grandson. I struggled with my faith and anger at God, but I continued to believe that He is in control.

For the past year, Sara, our older daughter, has been growing increasingly weak as her lungs succumbed to years of chronic

infections. Last September, Sara was accepted onto a lung transplant list. Today, I sit in an ICU waiting room, thanking God and
praying for the grieving family who lost someone so that my little
girl can breathe deeply. God is in control and answers prayer. I am
learning to accept that His ways are mysterious but true.

*"For my thoughts are not your thoughts, neither are your ways
my ways," declares the LORD. "As the heavens are higher than
the earth, so are my ways higher than your ways and my
thoughts than your thoughts"* (Isaiah 55:8-9).

*He performs wonders that cannot be fathomed, miracles that
cannot be counted. When he passes me, I cannot see him; when
he goes by, I cannot perceive him. If he snatches away, who can
stop him? Who can say to him, "What are you doing?"* (Job
9:10-12).

*Now we see but a poor reflection as in a mirror, then we shall
see face to face. Now I know in part; then I shall know fully,
even as I am fully known* (1 Corinthians 13:12).

*And the peace of God, which transcends all understanding,
will guard your hearts and your minds in Christ Jesus* (Philippians 4:7).

Angela Responds...

All through Scripture, the writers testify that in this life, we can
know God in part—"This is eternal life: that they may know you, the
only true God, and Jesus Christ, whom you have sent" (John 17:3)—
but we cannot know Him fully—"The secret things belong to the
LORD our God" (Deuteronomy 29:29).

God and His ways are mysterious to us. Certain things are not
revealed to us. Why would one family lose a son so tragically? Why
does one very sick daughter receive the gift of new life, but another
is lost? Who can fathom the mind of God or His purposes for them?

Reading this story, we are challenged by the family's generosity and their hearts of compassion for all the children they have been given. We grieve the loss of their son and then rejoice over the daughter's lung transplant. Picturing this mama, who has been through so much and now sits in the ICU waiting room, we scratch our heads and mutter to ourselves, "No one can understand the mysterious ways of God."

At the place where you and I encounter God's mystery, there is always a decision to be made. Will we choose doubt, or will we choose faith? Henry Blackaby has said, "When you can see, no faith is required." When you can see the answers and understand why with your mind, you don't need faith. You have full knowledge. But when you encounter the mysterious hand of God and His ways seem illogical to you, when you hurt because of loss and you wonder what in the world God was thinking, right there in your inability to understand, you will have to choose faith. And this is why faith is one of the essential components of the Christian life.

God is God, and we are not. Having faith means clinging to the promises of the Bible. "Faith is confidence in what we hope for and assurance about what we do not see" (Hebrews 11:1).

When we choose intentional faith over doubt, we are pleasing God. "Without faith it is impossible to please God, because anyone who comes to him must believe that he exists and that he rewards those who earnestly seek him" (Hebrews 11:6).

Maybe today the circumstances in your life make no sense. Maybe your heart is broken, and you cannot understand the ways of God. Faith is required to live this life because we are walking a road laid down by God. He is asking you and me to have faith, to trust in His goodness even if nothing good is in front of us, and to live our lives based on the truth of Romans 8:28: "We know that in all things God works for the good of those who love him."

We have limited comprehension of how God works, but as we humbly bow to His sovereignty, our faith increases. We learn more about what it means to worship a God who is above all things, to live for a God whose thoughts and ways transcend our ability to reason.

Faith means that we trust the God who promises to keep His

promises, the same God who says, "In this world you will have trouble, but take heart! I have overcome the world" (John 16:33). We intentionally choose to let our hearts be comforted by His wisdom and His love for us. He *is* the overcomer. He *does* have a plan and a purpose. We *do* see through a mirror dimly. His thoughts and ways *are* higher than ours.

And in the face of each mystery, we will choose faith, look to God, and passionately follow the encouragement of Proverbs 3:5-6: "Trust in the LORD with all your heart and lean not on your own understanding."

30

A PRAYER FOR
A PRODIGAL

From Sue...

My story is ongoing, a prayer yet unanswered but a hope that someday God will work a miracle.

My son, who is now 32, has abandoned his four children and is caught up in a world of drug addiction. I have not seen or heard from him for months. His children ask me every time I take care of them, "Have you seen my dad? Have you talked to him?" This has devastated the children and the whole family. Unfortunately, I have met too many grandparents struggling with the same problem. I do not understand the world of drugs and what they do to a mind, but I do know that my son used to be a loving father and a supportive son, but now he is gone.

My prayer is that like the prodigal son, he will "come to his senses" and see the Father waiting to bless him, forgive him, and adorn him with a robe and a ring. I long to talk to my son, to tell him I love him and plead with him to come home. Yet more than that, I want him to come back to the Lord and be the man of God he was called to be. I will continue to believe for this miracle.

Start children off on the way they should go, and even when they are old they will not turn from it (Proverbs 22:6).

But while he was still a long way off, his father saw him and was filled with compassion for him; he ran to his son, threw his arms around him and kissed him (Luke 15:20).

Matthew Responds...

Oh, how a heart of a parent aches for a child who is lost in this world. Perhaps you find yourself in the same painful place as Sue, sick to your stomach over the choices your child has made. Take comfort in this thought today: *God is committed to finding the lost.* He is pursuing your precious child today, even right now as you read this.

Throughout the Bible we receive powerful reminders of God's relentless pursuit of the lost. Jesus used the parable of the lost sheep to illustrate the value that heaven places on just one lost soul. "Suppose one of you has a hundred sheep and loses one of them. Doesn't he leave the ninety-nine in the open country and go after the lost sheep until he finds it?" (Luke 15:4).

Growing up, I used to love the Choose Your Own Adventure books. Maybe you remember them. These were stories written with multiple different endings. Throughout the book, the reader gets to decide which direction the story will go and how the adventure will end. I dug up one such book called *Monsters of the Deep*. A tagline for the book read, "Monsters aren't so scary when you're in control of the story."

But the same cannot be said about our real-life stories. When we decide to take control, well, that seems to be precisely when it *does* get scary. See, God loves us so much that He promises to pursue every lost soul on earth. But He also gives us the choice to choose our own adventures. We can follow His plan for our stories, or we can choose the same road the prodigal son did.

The youngest of two sons, the prodigal decided to cash in on his father's inheritance early and strike out on his own adventure. The word *prodigal* means recklessly wasteful. And that he was. The Scripture says he "squandered his wealth in wild living." At the wayward son's lowest point of desperation, though, memories of his father and his home came rushing back. The Scripture says, "He came to his senses." I'm a parent, and this is a part of the prodigal's story I find so encouraging. The Bible says, "Start children off on the way they should go, and even when they are old they will not turn from it." The prodigal demonstrated that when he came to his senses.

Maybe you were not a Christian while you were raising your children, and you worry that your prodigal wasn't started off on the way he or she should go. The Bible has so many promises to remind you of the power of prayer, including Psalm 91:15: "'Because he loves me,' declares the LORD, 'I will rescue him; I will protect him, for he acknowledges my name. He will call on me, and I will answer him.'" Prayer is a powerful thing. Don't stop lifting up your children in prayer.

Jim Cymbala, pastor of the Brooklyn Tabernacle, knows firsthand that prayer has the power to bring back a prodigal from darkness. In his book *Fresh Wind, Fresh Fire*, he tells of his daughter, who walked away from her parents and God for two and a half years. One Tuesday night, during a prayer meeting, the church joined together to pray exclusively for her. Thirty-two hours later, out of nowhere, Jim's daughter showed up at their house.

> As I came around the corner, I saw my daughter on the kitchen floor, rocking on her hands and knees, sobbing. Cautiously I spoke her name:
>
> "Chrissy?"
>
> She grabbed my pant leg and began pouring out her anguish.
>
> "Daddy—Daddy—I've sinned against God. I've sinned against myself. I've sinned against you and Mommy. Please forgive me—"
>
> My vision was as clouded by tears as hers. I pulled her up from the floor and held her close as we cried together.
>
> Suddenly she drew back. "Daddy," she said with a start, "*who was praying for me? Who was praying for me?*" Her voice was like that of a cross-examining attorney.

"What do you mean, Chrissy?"

"On Tuesday night, Daddy—who was praying for me?"*

At the very same time the church was lifting her up in prayer, God woke Chrissy up and spoke to her heart, and she returned to her family and to the Lord. God answers prayer. God pursues the prodigals. God rejoices over their return, as Henri Nouwen explains.

> God rejoices. Not because the problems of the world have been solved, not because all human pain and suffering have come to an end, nor because thousands of people have been converted and are now praising him for his goodness. No, God rejoices because *one* of his children who was lost has been found.†

There is no sweeter story than that of a prodigal returning home. Don't lose hope, and don't stop praying. Hold on until the day when you will be able to say what the prodigal father said as he ran out to meet his long-lost son: "Let's have a feast and celebrate. For this son of mine was dead and is alive again; he was lost and is found."

---

* Jim Cymbala, *Fresh Wind, Fresh Fire* (Grand Rapids: Zondervan, 1997), 65.

† Cited in Philip Yancey, *What's So Amazing About Grace?* (Grand Rapids: Zondervan, 1997), 53.

31

WHEN I AM NOT ENOUGH

From Shannon...

After having a beautiful baby boy, my husband and I decided not to pursue having any more biological children. (I have a disability that requires daily medication that is not conducive to safely carrying a child.) A year and a half later, feeling led to adopt, we opened our hearts and home to a five-month-old boy from Guatemala. The adoption process was supposed to take only four to nine months, but it drug on for more than two years. At two and a half, our Mark finally came home to us. Unfortunately, though, he was not unscathed. During his young, short life, he had already suffered from malnutrition, physical and emotional abuse, and severe neglect.

Left nearly crippled financially from the exhaustive adoption process, I personally struggled to bond with little Mark. His complex medical, cognitive, social, and emotional needs were overwhelming me. I finally realized that Jesus brought Mark to me for a reason, and the experience was either going to make me or break me.

It wasn't until I closed my eyes and opened my heart that I realized I was living a daily lesson in Christ's love for us. Every day I was given unique glimpses—windows into the nature of Christ and how God shows His love for us.

*Rejoice always, pray continually, give thanks in all circum-
stances; for this is God's will for you in Christ Jesus* (1 Thessalonians 5:16-18).

*My grace is sufficient for you, for my power is made perfect in
weakness* (2 Corinthians 12:9).

Angela Responds...

When I read Shannon's story, my heart broke for her family because
her story is also my brother's story. Seven years ago, my brother and
beautiful sister-in-law adopted sweet little Cole from an orphanage in
Russia. They had not been able to have children after trying for years
and felt that God very clearly led them to adopt. Their hearts were full.
All the funds were raised. After two trips to cold and snowy Russia, our
11-month-old little nephew, Cole, came home in their arms.

What began as an outpouring of compassion and love has become
seven years of incredible difficulty and pain for my brother and his wife.
Cole has manifested most of the problems that can be associated with
orphanage adoptions—attachment disorder, fetal alcohol syndrome,
and anger and control issues. It's just been so very hard. Every day, my
brother and his wife face trials that stretch them beyond what they
believe they can bear. Every day, they feel as if they are not enough.*

I asked my sister-in-law, "What do you cling to?"

She told me, "This journey has been so crazy and awful and good.
But the one thing that challenges me the most is God's instruction to
give thanks in all circumstances. In my sense of entitlement and when
I feel I should have something better, more peaceful, and easier, I am
challenged to the billionth degree to just give thanks. The bottom line
is, do I trust God? Will I thank Him even when I don't feel like it?"

Then she added, "I am constantly amazed that God thought that
I would be the best choice of a mom for Cole. He knew the countless
mistakes and failures I would make, but in His sovereignty, He still

---

* My brother began a foundation to assist other families with the often unanticipated costs of caring
  for adopted children. Please contact LifeChange Post Adoption Fund, Inc. for more information.

thought it was a good idea. I am so aware of my need for a Savior, and I am amazed at His grace for me when I am not enough."

I haven't adopted a difficult child—nothing close!—but for a hundred different reasons, I too have felt as if I am not enough. Probably you have too. And so how shall we live and respond and act when life is downright unrelenting, when it's so hard that nothing is going to change unless God shows up? I think we will have to do two things.

First, we will have to receive the grace God gives to the weak. His grace. His presence and moment-by-moment strength when we are absolutely sure we cannot take another step. Do you know what that feels like? Do you remember a time when you looked to heaven and yelled, "I can't do this!" But then, God gave you your next breath, your next ounce of strength, and your next instruction about what to do! Rarely does He reveal the whole plan—usually it's just the next portion we need.

Second, I truly believe we are supposed to give thanks, to worship in our weakness, to cry out to the sovereign God who is the Author and Architect of our lives. We are to bless Him in our lack, to thank Him for what we may never understand, trusting that He is working in our hearts, refining our character, and redirecting our paths. He is being glorified because we are sure that we are not enough. His power is being perfected because we are weak. His grace is being revealed because we have none.

Oh, my friend, where are you weak today? Where do your circumstances overwhelm you? Where are you absolutely sure you will never be enough? Let's bow our hearts across the altar of the only One who is able to see us through.

May His grace to you be sufficient and all that you need.

32

STRONG ENOUGH

From Tonia...

By the grace of God, I am the mother of three awesome children. It has always been them and me against the world.

I had my first daughter, Haleigh, when I was just a kid myself, at the age of 19. We grew up together. When she turned 19, she had a bad car accident after sliding on black ice, and she shattered her right leg. She was in the hospital on and off for months. Her health insurance was canceled because she couldn't maintain her full-time college status. She ended up having 11 surgeries as a result of this one freak car accident a mile from our house.

As a single parent and her mother, I never wanted to leave her side in the hospital. But while she slept, I would go home long enough to sleep a bit and take a quick shower. I remember feeling so incredibly alone. My family was a great support. They were there as much as could be, but at night, when the lights were out, I would lie in my bed and just cry from the loneliness. I was exhausted both emotionally and physically.

The accident was three years ago, and she is still recovering. She still has a long road of surgeries and physical therapy ahead of her. Once, when I was with her in the hospital, I said to her, "Haleigh, the Lord doesn't put anything on us that He doesn't think we are strong enough to handle."

She replied, "Well, He must think I'm pretty freakin' strong!"

If not for my faith, I would have gone out of my mind. Through it all, I have never felt as if God left my side. He guided me to do what was necessary to protect my daughter. I thank God for my kids every single day.

I can do all this through him who gives me strength (Philippians 4:13).

He gives strength to the weary and increases the power of the weak... Those who hope in the LORD will renew their strength. They will soar on wings like eagles; they will run and not grow weary, they will walk and not be faint (Isaiah 40:29,31).

With man this is impossible, but with God all things are possible (Matthew 19:26).

Matthew Responds...

I don't even need to ask if you have ever faced an impossible circumstance. We all will at some point in our lives. Perhaps you are facing one right now. Today, you may be staring down a struggle that seems much bigger than you are, wondering how in the world you are going to make it through. As I read this single mother's heartbreaking story about her and her daughter's hardships, I pictured both Tonia and Haleigh standing at the foot of a mile-high mountain, one that was way too tall for them to climb on their own strength.

Theirs is a trial of traumatic proportions. Tonia was trying to be strong for her daughter, trying to encourage her not to lose hope, when she reminded her, "The Lord doesn't put anything on you that He doesn't think you are strong enough to handle." Meanwhile, Haleigh, a frustrated teenager whose dreams of a college degree seemed to be slipping beyond her reach, was struggling to see any hope in her mom's encouragement. I was struck by Haleigh's angst-ridden response. It was so real, so human, and so relatable. "Well, He must think I'm pretty freakin' strong!"

Can you relate to Haleigh's emotional response, her lack of faith? I know I can. In my own way, in the middle of my own trials, I have doubted my own strength and questioned God's plan. I have had my share of moments when, standing on the edge of the unknown, I *was* certain of one thing—God had the wrong guy for the job. Mother Teresa once said something like this: "I know God will not give me anything I can't handle. I just wish that He didn't trust me so much."

My mom loves to tell the story of a time when I struggled to see how I could possibly be strong enough for a particular task at hand. She tells me that when I was in preschool, the teacher informed my parents that I needed to be able to tie my shoes by a certain date. I was frustrated as my mom tried to practice with me. I would prop my foot up on a chair, take one shoestring end in each hand, and try and try to no avail. I tied one tangled knot after another.

Mom says I grew more and more frustrated, afraid I might never learn how to tie my shoes. My dad tried to encourage me by telling me to repeat Matthew 19:26 after him: "With God all things are possible."

In response, a discouraged and skeptical five year-old version of me repeated, "With God all things *should* be possible!"

Aren't you glad that Scripture from Matthew doesn't read the way *this* Matthew thought it did? I know I am. I love the certainty in this Scripture. *All* things, not some things. *Are* possible, not should be possible. And how can this Scripture hold such confidence, such certainty? One need look no further than the first two words: "With God." The confidence in this Scripture comes from its source of certainty—an unfailing, unchanging God.

Regardless of how many tangled knots you are holding in your hands right now, you too can know that God is the only true source of certainty in this life. God promises that He can make a way and help you climb what you once saw as your unscalable mountain.

The Bible is filled with powerful pointers to our true source of strength (which is a good thing, because I need daily reminders). Another Scripture that has brought me confidence in the face of trials is one that I hope will encourage you wherever you find yourself today: "I can do all this through him who gives me strength" (Philippians 4:13). Again, notice that the confidence in this verse comes from our only true source of certainty in this life, Christ.

I find it interesting that Paul wrote those words while he was in prison. See, Paul was not foolish enough to believe that he alone was capable of doing the impossible. But drawing from his true source of certainty and placing his confidence in Christ, he spoke these words with the conviction of one who had seen a great God do impossible things in his life.

When your own strength finally fails, and it will, you can be confident in the strength of an unfailing God. Let the weight of your impossible circumstance be lifted off your shoulders. Truth is, you just aren't strong enough to carry your story on your own. But here's the best part—you don't have to be.

33

THE BEST WORST THING

Matthew's Story...

I've got two scars, one on my arm and one on my throat. Both scars tell a story, and both have shaped the story I tell. They represent two different trials that threatened my ability to pursue my musical dreams.

In 2002, I was offered a record deal. I was ecstatic! I had worked so hard for this opportunity, and it had finally arrived. However, just two weeks before signing on the dotted line, I suffered a freak accident, falling through a window at my house. The broken glass severed an artery in my left arm, and after five days in the hospital and complications with surgery, the prognosis was less than positive. The doctors said I had extensive nerve damage and might not regain full strength or feeling in my hand.

I'm a guitar and piano player, so this news was a devastating blow. In a split second I had gone from the doorstep of a dream to the den of disappointment. Forget signing a record deal—I couldn't even tie my own shoe! But God was so faithful during that season of my story. I could sense that He was going to use this trial to prepare my heart for the season ahead. After six months of physical therapy, I slowly began to pick up the guitar again. I never regained all of the feeling in my left hand, but I can play the guitar, and the scar that runs the length of my left arm makes for a good excuse when I play a bad chord!

Fast-forward five years. Same hospital, same patient. Only this time, the surgery was on my vocal cords. Doctors said it was a last-ditch attempt to repair my damaged voice (news no singer ever wants to hear). On May 17, 2007, I had surgery on my throat, wondering if I had possibly sung my last song. Ironically, I was supposed to be in the recording studio working on a new CD titled *Something to Say*. Instead, I was in lying in a hospital bed, and for the next several months I would have *nothing* to say.

After the surgery, I was unable to speak or sing for many weeks, and I used a dry erase board to communicate. At times the uncertainty of not knowing if my voice would come back was unbearable. I spent weeks in solitude and silence, pouring my heart out to God. I spent another six months having to relearn how to sing—a humbling experience. But God healed my voice and once again showed me that He wasn't done with my story.

I used to think these two chapters from my story were the worst things that ever happened to me. These days I step onstage as a singer with some scars, and I smile as I catch a glimpse of what God has been up to all along. My scars keep me humble. My scars show the world who healed me. And somehow those worst things…well, they've become the best things that ever happened to me because I have seen God use them in my life and in the lives of other people.

Consider it pure joy, my brothers and sisters, whenever you face trials of many kinds, because you know that the testing of your faith produces perseverance. Let perseverance finish its work so that you may be mature and complete, not lacking anything (James 1:2-4).

What has happened to me has actually served to advance the gospel…It has become clear…that I am in chains for Christ (Philippians 1:12-13).

Matthew Responds...

Oh, where have you gone, perspective? Perspective is a fair-weather friend if there ever was one. When our stories seem to be going the way we hoped they would, perspective makes a grand entrance, and we boldly proclaim, "God is so good!" But when our circumstances take a turn for the worse, when we face a trial or an injury or the loss of a job, when our joy is challenged by pain, perspective always tries to catch the first train out of town, leaving our hearts searching for one good reason why this bad thing is happening to us.

One Sunday morning after my vocal cord surgery, I reluctantly attended church (at my wife's request). I like church. I really do. I just hated the thought of standing there silent while the people around me lifted their voices in worship. I saw it as just another reminder that my voice had been taken from me. But I went anyway, and as the pastor began his message, I immediately felt as if he were talking straight to me.

"Today's message is entitled, 'Why Does God Allow Bad Things to Happen to Good People,'" he said. This was the question that had been swimming around in my mind for a few weeks. I was a good person. I just could not understand why this was happening to me and why God wasn't healing me faster. The pastor went on to read a quote by C.S. Lewis: "God whispers to us in our pleasures, speaks in our conscience, but shouts in our pains: it is His megaphone to rouse a deaf world."

And there it was! The perspective that had gone missing in the midst of my adversity came rushing back to me as I realized God was trying to get my attention. He was inviting to me to leave my little pity party behind and to consider instead that He had a purpose for my scars. Suddenly my question switched from "Why, God?" to "What are You up to, God?"

John Piper wrote, "The deepest need that you and I have in weakness and adversity is not quick relief, but the well-grounded confidence that what is happening to us is part of the greatest purpose in the universe."

Paul wrote the book of Philippians while he was in prison for sharing the gospel. But even in prison, Paul had an unshakeable joy. How? Paul's faith in Christ provided him with an eternal perspective. He wrote, "What has happened to me has really served to advance the gospel…It has become clear…that I am in chains for Christ." Paul knew God was up to something. He knew God could turn any circumstance, whether joyful or painful, into an opportunity for the world to witness His glory.

Paul went on to say, "Because of my chains, most of the brothers and sisters have become confident in the Lord and dare all the more to proclaim the gospel without fear." God does not promise an escape from weakness or adversity. "For it has been granted to you on behalf of Christ not only to believe in him, but also to suffer for him" (Philippians 1:29). He does, however, promise strength and joy to endure our most difficult days. If you allow God to get your attention, He will use your adversity to show you many things. He will use your scars to shape you into the person He wants you to become. Then, watch in amazement as He transforms the worst things that ever happened to you into your best opportunities to minister to others.

Rick Warren wrote, "If you want God to bless you and use you greatly, you must be willing to walk with a limp the rest of your life, because God uses weak people…Other people are going to find healing in your wounds. Your greatest life messages and your most effective ministry will come out of your deepest hurts." Your pain is God's megaphone. He's trying to get your attention. Look to Him. In time He will reveal the purpose of your scars. And as He shows you His plan, don't be surprised to find that the worst things that happened to you in life were the best things after all.

34

A MOTHER'S LOVE

From Debbie...

My life has suddenly taken an unimaginable turn. I have no way of knowing how to walk this path I find myself on now.

Just two days ago my 22-year-old son was sentenced to four years in prison. Why? There's no simple answer, but the bottom line is that he is a drug addict. Of course, there are now many consequences and complications in our situation, and I by no means excuse his actions or deny his guilt, but I can say with a heavy heart that the punishment does not fit the crime. You may not believe this, but Andrew is a good kid. He's friendly, he's personable, and he has a heart of gold.

Here is my dilemma: How does a mother like me mend her broken heart for a son who is away? How do I calm the fear of all the what-ifs that lurk in the back of my mind? How do I hold my family together and continue to build those memories that bind a family together without Andrew?

I know God has a perfect plan. I also know I don't have to understand it or like it, but I must accept it. I must trust Him and hold on to the faith and hope He offers. But my pain is real, and it is raw. I feel as if I have a gaping wound that only the loving balm of Christ can heal. I am not angry at God, nor do I feel abandoned, but I do feel alone. I can't hear Him or feel Him. Isn't this the time when

He will pick me up and carry me through this valley? I want to find joy in this tragedy and grow deeper in my relationship with Christ.

Love is patient, love is kind. It does not envy, it does not boast, it is not proud. It does not dishonor others, it is not self-seeking, it is not easily angered, it keeps no record of wrongs. Love does not delight in evil but rejoices with the truth. It always protects, always trusts, always hopes, always perseveres (1 Corinthians 13:4-7).

Above all, love each other deeply, because love covers over a multitude of sins (1 Peter 4:8).

Angela Responds...

This morning I had the great privilege of speaking to about 200 young moms. They were the cutest bunch of ponytailed, tired women you've ever seen. Some of them had dropped off their children at the provided nursery, but many of them held their sleeping babies or carried them in their comfy car seats. Some stood at the back and quietly swayed with the wiggly ones.

I talked to them about God's love. "He sees. God sees you stumble through the night to care for the ones He has given to you. He sees the sacrifices you make. He knows the depth of your love and concern. Your love and work is not invisible to Him. God sees all that you give, and He is so very pleased." But I wanted them to know about more than God's love. I also wanted them to know about the grace that God so lavishly gives to mamas—the wannabe perfect ones, the "I know I'm imperfect" ones, and the ones who never think they will be enough. The entire journey of parenthood is about learning to give and receive the grace of God—a gracious love that reflects His love to us.

Gracious love enables a mother to look into the eyes of her child who's made mistakes and still see all that is good. That kind of love doesn't deride or berate children for their foolishness, immaturity, mistakes, bad decisions, or sin. Instead, real love, without trying to hide the truth, gently puts issues to rest in the goodness and forgiveness of Christ.

If I could sit with Debbie and share my heart with her, here's what I might say.

> My sweet sister, you have given God's gracious and forgiving love to your son. Now you must receive it for your own. The powerful grace and love of God will heal your heart and quiet your fears. He has you, a beautiful mom and son, right in the palm of His hand. Nothing has changed about His love for you. God watched you rock your sweet little baby all those years ago, and today, He sees you still. He sees the sacrifices you have made. He hears you praying through the night for the one He entrusted to you. He knows the depth of your wounds, and He longs to give His gracious, healing love to you.
>
> Prison may hold your son for a season, but it does not isolate him from the gracious love of God. God's love knows no boundaries. Prison walls cannot keep God's grace from your son, and that prison does not distance God from the rest of your family. Our God is a saving Father who breaks the chains of sin and mends the hearts of broken people. A mother's love is a powerful force, but even more fierce is God's love for you.
>
> Debbie, God has you. Sometimes our numb hearts cannot feel His presence. Many days, our human sadness cannot muster up a joy. But God has not moved. You are His and He is yours. God *always* comes to rescue His beloved.*

If you are numb with grief, if you have a really good child who has made some dumb mistakes, if you are a prisoner who is experiencing the consequences of your own choices, or if you are simply angry and wandering and tired, would you hear today the truth of God's love for you?

God's love never fails.

---

* To learn more about resources for inmates and their families, please visit www.speakupforhope.org.

35

THE HEALING HAS BEGUN

From Ginny...

One of the worst decisions I ever made was 35 years ago at the age of 18. I became pregnant and decided not to keep the child. I was too afraid and ashamed to go to my parents for help, so I decided to fix my mistake and terminate the pregnancy. I still remember climbing the stairs in the clinic with a group of other young women.

I have always been sorry that I did not seek out other options, and I have often thought of how my life would be different if I would have chosen to give life.

That was 35 years ago. But today I have hope! I know God has forgiven me and I will meet my child one day in heaven. I made a poor choice in 1975, but today I have hope and a strong conviction to lead children to Christ at an early age by working with children's ministries at my church.

He heals the brokenhearted and binds up their wounds (Psalm 147:3).

"He himself bore our sins" in his body on the tree, so that we might die to sins and live for righteousness; "by his wounds you have been healed" (1 Peter 2:24).

Matthew Responds...

"I don't want you to think I have it all together." That is what Ginny said to me when I spoke with her on the phone to tell her I read her story. "I'm still working through my past and told my husband about my abortion only two weeks ago." Until she sent me her story, Ginny had kept this painful part of her past a secret even from those closest to her. After she found out I had written a song inspired by her story, she worked up the courage to open up and tell her husband of 20 years about this shadow in her past. She seemed determined to make sure I didn't have the wrong idea about her. "I'm still working through all of this," she said, "but finally sharing my story has been a huge part of the healing process."

Like Ginny, so many of the people who sent their stories to me chose not to tell me about the best days of their lives. They left out the details of their college graduation day, their 401(k)s, or their first kiss. They didn't write to tell me about vacations to Disney World or the day they got a puppy. No, when asked to write down their story, when asked to talk about defining moments in their lives, the vast majority of people chose to share with me from their most broken chapters.

What are the broken chapters? The broken chapters are the ones we wish were never written. They are the pages filled with the parts of our stories we desperately wish we could go back and rewrite. They are the chapters that you would rip right out of the book if you could. But you know you can't, so the safest option often seems to be locking them up and hiding them away. If it were up to us, no one would ever read the broken chapters from our stories. No one would ever discover how broken we really are.

Ginny had done just that for many years before deciding the time had come. Time to tell her story, broken chapters and all. So did thousands of other people. No more holding it in or hiding it away. Ginny and all the others are just honest people who are courageous enough to stand up and take a step toward healing by saying, "This is part of my story." And in doing this, they are choosing to be willing—willing to allow God to use even these broken chapters in hopes that they can give Him glory and help someone else.

Throughout the course of our stories, we will all wind up with our share of broken chapters. "All have sinned and fall short of the glory of God" (Romans 3:23). We are born broken people. Some broken chapters we write for ourselves because of the choices we make. Some are written for us by circumstances beyond our control—the sad result of living in a fallen world. Perhaps as you are reading this, you find yourself thinking about your own broken chapters, whatever they may be. The greatest mistakes you've ever made. The parts of your past or even your present that you're ashamed of. What have you done with them? Have you dealt with them? Has the healing already begun in your life, or have you, like so many others, chosen to bury your brokenness, your guilt, and your shame down as deep as you can?

Remember today that even though you may be able to hide your broken chapters from your friends or even your family, nothing can be hidden from God. "I the LORD search the heart and examine the mind" (Jeremiah 17:10). Your Creator knows everything there is to know about you. "You have searched me, LORD, and you know me" (Psalm 139:1). In fact, your broken chapters are precisely the reason why He came to earth and died on a cross. "For the son of Man came to seek and to save the lost" (Luke 19:10). Jesus died on a cross for our sins, and with His nail-scarred hands, He held out the hope of healing to all. "By his wounds you have been healed" (1 Peter 2:24).

Your healing begins the moment you turn your eyes toward a Savior who loves you, and choose to accept this gift of healing grace. Your healing continues as you allow God to work in those broken chapters of your story, showing you His plan for your life. As you open up to a life with no secrets, He opens up doors and uses your brokenness to draw others to Him. And like Ginny, whose painful past has led her to a passion for working with children, you may be amazed to discover how God can turn *your* greatest pain into a passion.

Healing is a process, and I for one can relate with Ginny when she said, "I don't want you to think I have it all together." No one has it all together. As long as we are living this side of heaven, we will be healing works in progress. But if we choose to embrace God's forgiveness in our lives, we can be certain that someday, when we stand before the Lord, our healing will be complete.

So here we are. This is where the rubber meets the road. What will you do with your broken chapter? Don't you long to find healing? Aren't you tired of carrying that secret around with you? You don't have to do that anymore. Just as Jesus lifted Ginny out from under the weight of her 35-year-old secret, Jesus is looking at you and whispering an invitation. "I love you. I forgive you. Now, give Me your broken chapter and let the healing begin."

36

THE FAMILY OF GOD

From Frannie...

"I want out of this family or I will end it all," I told my social worker. A victim of years of mental and physical abuse, I had cut myself and tried to "end it all" before. If someone had told me I was as worthless as a lump of coal, I would have believed that. I never would have believed myself to be a "diamond in the rough."

I was born unwanted. My birth father left when he found out my mother was pregnant. I didn't see him until I was 14.

Being raised by an overwhelmed, illiterate mother and stepfather was anything but pleasant. I used survival skills to cope—fighting, swearing, talking back, manipulation. But at age 9, I began attending a Salvation Army church. I escaped my difficult home life by going to the Army building every time the doors were open. I attended Sunday school, morning and evening worship, Bible studies, prayer meetings, and youth activities.

I briefly moved in with my birth father when he reappeared in my life, and then I lived with one of his ex-wives. With four other teens in that household, some sexually active, my home life was about as bad as it could get. At this point, I tried to take my own life and ended up in a mental health facility.

I prayed desperately and cried out for help. It came in the form of a visit from a Salvation Army captain named Cheriann and a social worker. The social worker pointed out that the only positive thing in my life was the Salvation Army. She asked Cheriann if anyone in the church could take me in and care for me.

Cheriann and her husband, Kevin, could think of no family in their congregation that might be an option. Then Cheriann suggested to Kevin that they take me into their home as their daughter. Kevin immediately said, "No! We've just adopted a boy who is now four years old. How can we care for a sixteen-year-old?"

"But," he added, "I will pray about it."

God quickly answered that prayer; one week later, on January 23, 1999, I became a part of their family.

Soon I discovered that I was part of a real family. Four-year-old Arthur loved having a big sister, and nights around the dinner table instilled in me a clearer concept of God's love and acceptance. For the first time, I began to trust people and to feel wanted and loved. In addition to my new parents and a brother, I now had loving grandparents, aunts, uncles, and cousins, as well as caring teachers, counselors, and social workers.

I graduated from the community college with an associate's degree in family and child development. Following graduation, I worked at a day-care center and assisted at one of the Army's camps. I am still growing spiritually.

My future plans are not crystal clear, but God is working in my life. I definitely want to touch people's lives, especially teenagers, and let them know that there is hope if they trust in God. God may be leading me to be an officer in the Salvation Army.

Without the love, prayers, and help of so many of God's people, I would be a very different young woman today.

Dear friends, let us love one another, for love comes from God.
Everyone who loves has been born of God and knows God.

*Whoever does not love does not know God, because God is love.
This is how God showed his love among us: He sent his one and
only Son into the world that we might live through him. This
is love: not that we loved God, but that he loved us and sent his
Son as an atoning sacrifice for our sins. Dear friends, since God
so loved us, we also ought to love one another* (1 John 4:7-11).

*Consequently, you are no longer foreigners and strangers, but
fellow citizens with God's people and members of his household* (Ephesians 2:19).

Angela Responds...

Frannie's story is the kind of story that should be shouted from
the tallest building. Her news should be run with a bold-letter headline in papers around the world. It should be posted on Facebook and
retweeted until the all tweets run out. The love of God radically and
powerfully transforms lives! Really and truly. Amazingly and mirac-
ulously. The love of God, poured through the faithful lives of godly
people, changes everything!

Can you imagine the broken path of Frannie's childhood? You may
have walked a similar path. You may live in that kind of brokenness
this very day. I love that at nine years old, this little girl who lived such
a toxic life began to crave the beautiful, healthy love she encountered at
the Salvation Army. God's love. God's goodness. God's grace and compassion and mercy. Frannie met Jesus at the Salvation Army, and His
love for her brought a healing that can't be found anywhere else on earth.

So many families struggle with dysfunction, abuse, and addiction.
Children are wounded, and eventually they become adults who continue to make the choices that seem familiar to them. They walk the
same hurtful path, introducing yet another generation to brokenness
and pain.

But there is another family for all who give their hearts to Jesus
Christ. It's the family of God. Becoming a follower of Jesus means you
are no longer an outcast or a stranger to the fellowship of believers.
You belong to God. You have a home here on this earth and a home

forever as a citizen of heaven. You are God's child, and no one can ever take that away.

Maybe you've never lived anywhere you felt safe. Maybe rejection and disappointment are parts of your story too. Maybe all your life, you have longed for a healthy love, only to decide it can't be found on this earth. I have such great, great news for you. The love of God is the love you can count on. And God is not only faithful but also able to transform you with His powerful love. Really. God comes to you when you call on His name, and He changes every place you will allow Him to work. What He has done for Frannie, He will do for you!

I want to invite you to come. Come to Jesus. Come to the family of God, where His love is changing all of us from the embarrassing people we have been into a more beautiful reflection of who He is. We are not a perfect bunch, our family, but God is a perfect God, and we follow Him. We're learning how to love the way He loves. We want to give you the compassion He has so freely given to us. We want you to know the only One who is able to take a toxic life and transform every single piece for His glory.

Welcome to the family!

37

LONGING FOR HEAVEN

From Amy...

I'd like to share Isaac's story. Born on March 13, 2003, he was a precious Hispanic-Caucasian baby born to a mother who couldn't care for him. We were blessed to be there at his birth and take him home from the hospital. We officially adopted him nine months later. He immediately brought joy beyond words to our family.

But Isaac had difficulty developing like other babies. He didn't sit up on his own or crawl within the normal developmental milestones. His speech was delayed. By December 2005, Isaac was in the hospital and diagnosed with a rare blood disorder called hemophagocytic lymphohistiocytosis (HLH).

The disease took his eyesight, ravaged his central nervous system, and left him brain damaged and unable to breathe without a ventilator. After battling the disease for 11 months, God took him home. He was just three years old.

But Isaac's story is so much bigger than just his three years. In the short time he was alive, and for the 11 months he was sick, he touched many lives. Our small town rallied around our family during this time. Many heard his story and our story of faith. For a while, I wondered why he had to die. I thought maybe there was someone in our city or state that needed to hear his story. And I know there were—many people told us how Isaac had touched them in one way or another.

But I also realized that Isaac's death had done something to me. I now long for heaven like never before. I am now waiting for the sky to break open and for Jesus to come back for me. I want to see Jesus, and I want to see Isaac again. Isaac's death has also opened our hearts to other children with medical needs. Because of Isaac, three foster children live with us, including one who was a shaken baby.

The ripple effects of Isaac's death are being felt even today. Even though he lived just three short years, his legacy will live on in the foster children we bring into our home and in our hope and longing for heaven.

Our citizenship is in heaven (Philippians 3:20).

We know that if the earthly tent we live in is destroyed, we have a building from God, an eternal house in heaven, not built by human hands. Meanwhile we groan, longing to be clothed instead with our heavenly dwelling (2 Corinthians 5:1-2).

Yet I am always with you; you hold me by my right hand. You guide me with your counsel, and afterward you will take me into glory. Whom have I in heaven but you? And earth has nothing I desire besides you. My flesh and my heart may fail, but God is the strength of my heart and my portion forever (Psalm 73:23-26).

Angela Responds...

When someone you love goes to heaven before you, so much changes. Heaven means even more because the one you love is there. Amy has a son in heaven. I have a sister and grandparents in heaven. And now when I think of heaven, I have two yearnings. It's the home of Jesus, whom I can't wait to see. And it's the place where the people I have loved on this earth are waiting for me.

Randy Alcorn has said, "Our longing for heaven is a longing for

God." When we long for heaven, we are longing for everything to be made right. To be with our Savior and the saints who have led us to God. To be in the home we were made for, with perfected bodies and perfected hearts. And to be surrounded by the ones we love, living in fellowship and joy for all eternity. When I stop for just a moment, I can feel my soul longing to go where it was made to be. This earth is not really my home, and my soul longs for its home in heaven.

But what if our longings and aches are supposed to teach us how to live these days on earth a little differently? What if this longing for God can remind us to reframe our earthly desires? Keeping eternity in view can teach us to passionately keep our eyes on God and make the choices that will matter for all eternity. Amy's glimpse of eternity prompted her to make big heart decisions to care for foster children with special needs. She's doing what matters and what will still matter in a million years. She is alive and intentional and loving well for the glory of God.

But what about you and me? Will we read Amy's story and turn the page, or will we let her understanding of heaven transform the way we live each day? Until we step into eternity, will we live for ourselves and for this one moment, or will we ask God how to make our time matter?

Building into eternity will look different for each one of us. We are each given different gifts and abilities. Each one is called to different places and groups. But today, this very day, what would it mean for you to live with an eternal perspective? How would you change this day if you choose to live with heaven in mind? Maybe it means you take the afternoon off and surprise your wife with coffee and conversation. Maybe it means you make the call you've been putting off. Or that you give mercy where you've been withholding it. Or you stop talking and start doing. Or maybe you're the one who is supposed to sell everything and go love some people in Africa.

However God directs you, I think this longing for heaven is about living in obedience while we're still on this earth. With every moment, the Holy Spirit is faithful to tell us which way to walk or stop or wait. The question is, with eternity in mind, will we obey? Will we choose to do what matters and decide to pass by the trivial and distracting?

If your citizenship is in heaven, and if heaven is where you were made to be, wouldn't it make sense to start living now the way you'll live there?

What will matter in heaven? God's answer to you will show you how you should live here.

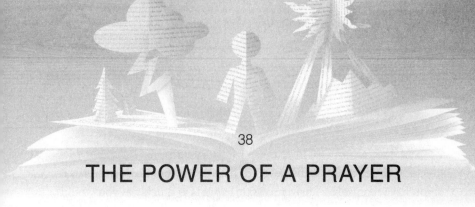

38

THE POWER OF A PRAYER

From Gerson...

Hello, my name is Gerson and I just turned 13.

Life used to be hard because my father was not a Christian but my mom was. Sometimes they would fight and yell, and I would just stand in a corner, crying. About two years ago my pastor asked the whole church to start praying for 24 hours. So I wrote down on a whiteboard what I wanted to pray about and these are the exact words I wrote: My father to be a Christian.

All of a sudden people started to pray about my father. Two months later, my pastor went to talk with my family and especially my dad, and man, what a talk! That very night, my dad accepted Christ in his heart. My mom and my little bro cried for joy and I just praised God with all my heart. My dad and I have been baptized in water, and we talk a lot about our God. I just hope the devil never destroys my family ever again. My brother loves reading the Bible to my father and he is the best brother I will ever have. Now that is the story of my life.

The prayer of a righteous person is powerful and effective (James 5:16).

In every situation, by prayer and petition, with thanksgiving, present your requests to God (Philippians 4:6).

Be still, and know that I am God (Psalm 46:10).

Matthew Responds...

Do you ever doubt the power of prayer? Maybe you don't feel as if you have received an answer to your requests as quickly as you would like. Ever find yourself wondering, "Does this really work? Does God really hear me when I call on Him?" Sometimes in our journeys of faith, our prayers seem to do little more than bounce off the ceiling, leaving us doubt-filled and faithless.

Still no job on the horizon.

Still no sign of your prodigal child.

Still no good report from your doctor.

The psalms remind us that the only way to survive these "still no..." seasons is to "be still and know" that He is God and that He hears us when we pray. If we abide by this instruction, we will see the power of prayer at work with our own eyes and in His perfect timing. Many who have gone before us have experienced the power of a prayer. Consider Peter in prison.

> Peter was kept in prison, but the church was earnestly praying to God for him.
>
> The night before Herod was to bring him to trial, Peter was sleeping between two soldiers, bound with two chains, and sentries stood guard at the entrance. Suddenly an angel of the Lord appeared and a light shone in the cell. He struck Peter on the side and woke him up. "Quick, get up!" he said, and the chains fell off Peter's wrists (Acts 12:5-7).

The sick woman experienced the power of prayer when she crawled through a crowd just to touch Jesus' garment.

> And a woman was there who had been subject to bleeding for twelve years. She had suffered a great deal under the care of many doctors and had spent all she had, yet instead

of getting better she grew worse. When she heard about Jesus, she came up behind him in the crowd and touched his cloak, because she thought, "If I just touch his clothes, I will be healed." Immediately her bleeding stopped and she felt in her body that she was freed from her suffering.

At once Jesus realized that power had gone out from him. He turned around in the crowd and asked, "Who touched my clothes?"

"You see the people crowding against you," his disciples answered, "and yet you can ask, 'Who touched me?'"

But Jesus kept looking around to see who had done it. Then the woman, knowing what had happened to her, came and fell at his feet and, trembling with fear, told him the whole truth. He said to her, "Daughter, your faith has healed you. Go in peace and be freed from your suffering."

The dying thief on the cross experienced the power of prayer when he reached out for forgiveness with his last breaths.

Then he said, "Jesus, remember me when you come into your kingdom."

Jesus answered him, "Truly I tell you, today you will be with me in paradise" (Luke 23:42-43).

And if you need to be encouraged by one more example of the power of prayer today, go back and reread Gerson's story once more. With the faith of a child, this boy simply made his request known to God, believing that his prayer would be answered. And guess what? God heard his prayer and answered. What a defining moment in the story of this young boy's life! A moment he will always be able to point to, remembering how the power of a prayer helped to restore his family.

No matter how long your "still no…" list may be today, ask God to help you simply "be still and know" that He is God. In His perfect timing, all of your "still no…" situations will have their answers. And the story of your life will be living proof that prayer is a powerful thing.

39

JUST FOR TODAY

From Galyn...

Aspen is my middle child. After she was born, she was kept in the PICU at Phoenix Children's Hospital. When Aspen was a week old, she was scheduled to go for her first open-heart surgery. But when a procedure backfired, she crashed. The doctors and nurses worked all day trying to stabilize her. Even though they succeeded, Aspen was a vegetable. She had already had a ventricular brain hemorrhage, but when she crashed it spread to her whole brain. She was on a ventilator and was completely unresponsive. So when Aspen was two weeks old, we felt God was leading us to put her in His hands and remove life support.

Doctors told us that Aspen died three times that night, and God alone sent her back each time. After the third time, Aspen stabilized, and she started waking up the very next day!

Aspen has since had four open-heart surgeries and several other surgeries. It's now been over six years since Aspen was born. Since day one, doctors have told me more times than I care to remember that Aspen is dying. She is a beautiful child of God who is in kindergarten, learning to read, loves math, and picks her own lunch each day. She is the best-looking vegetable I have ever seen! I have no idea how long I have Aspen for; I honestly believe

God told me He is going to take her home. But until that day finally comes, I will enjoy her every day I get.

This is the day which the LORD has made; let us rejoice and be glad in it (Psalm 118:24 NASB).

Do not worry about tomorrow, for tomorrow will worry about itself. Each day has enough trouble of its own (Matthew 6:34).

I have learned to be content whatever the circumstances. I know what it is to be in need, and I know what it is to have plenty. I have learned the secret of being content in any and every situation (Philippians 4:11-12).

Angela Responds...

Here are my favorite lines from this story: "She is the best-looking vegetable I have ever seen! I have no idea how long I have Aspen for... But until that day finally comes, I will enjoy her every day I get."

Amen and amen. I pray that the days for Aspen multiply into years and then abundantly healthy decades. But oh my, I am so touched by the tone of her mother. Can you hear that there is something genuinely different about the way she writes? This mom has walked through six of the most difficult years anyone could ever imagine. Time after time, she was told her daughter was dying. Time after time, the circumstances seemed to confirm death was near. And yet six-year-old Aspen goes to kindergarten and thrives! And Aspen's faith journey has changed that mama forever.

If we sat down for coffee with this family, I bet they could give us a long list of spiritual lessons they've learned these past six years. And probably in most of those lessons, their hearts cried out to God in pain. "I didn't want to learn this. Not now, not so fast." In just the few paragraphs of their story, they demonstrate such a spiritual maturity for us all to emulate. Maybe some of their spiritual lessons would go something like this.

1. *Our daughter belongs to God.* He gave her life. He knew her before she was. He carefully entrusted her to us because He believed we could love her best. She is God's baby girl, and we have learned that the span of her life will not be decided by us or by doctors or medicines or machines. God knows exactly how long to leave His daughter in our arms.

2. *We have learned to live in the grace God provides for this one day.* (Oh, that I could remember that beautiful lesson and live consistently in its truth!) Today is the day the Lord has made. God gives us enough grace for today—there is grace enough for today's problems, today's testing, today's challenge. All God asks is that we live today for His glory, that we spend this day beautifully relying on Him, trusting what we cannot understand, believing that the heart of God is for us. He is Father, He is wisdom, and He is peace. And all that He is, is sufficient for today. Tomorrow is not for us to worry about.

3. *God has taught us contentment regardless of the circumstances.* When everything seems out of control and nothing we do for Aspen seems to work, God is still on the throne of heaven and in control of all that concerns us. I imagine this hard-won lesson probably came after years of emotional battle. Can you imagine how badly they have wanted to have answers? Healing? Hope? But probably a day of surrender finally came when this family could make their confession of faith to God. "We trust You. Regardless of the circumstances, we trust You. Our contentment will come from the peace of trusting You." Contentment in any circumstance is the mark of great spiritual maturity.

4. *God has given us joy.* Oh, that it would be the same for you and me, that you and I would rejoice in all things! In my house we say, "It's all grace." I bet they say that a lot in Aspen's house too. When you realize that all you have has come to you by grace, you have an opportunity to live in the joy that grace brings. I pray that we would look for the

moments of joy regardless of the circumstances. I also pray that we would be able to give to others a joy they have not yet learned how to find.

I am so grateful to Aspen's family for sharing their story and their lessons and inspiring us to live this day with contentment, trust, and fullness of joy. I won't soon forget the story of the best-looking vegetable ever. And I'm sure I'll smile every time I remember.

40

THE PURSUIT OF
SO-CALLED PERFECTION

From Esther Lee...

I am Korean-American. I have never, not even once, thought I was pretty or attractive. While growing up, the girls around me were so much more beautiful and always had guys hanging around them. It also didn't help that I wore thick glasses throughout elementary and junior high school, which made me a target for kids to make fun of. I stayed away from the popular kids and hung out with other quiet friends. I've had this self-consciousness while growing up, and now I am a junior in college.

Recently, I finally just gave all of my insecurities over to God, and I felt Him wash them all away. He told me that I was beautiful and that He created me the way that I am, the way I look. Our Father is *perfect*, flawless...He makes no mistakes. He made me the way I am, and He, having no flaws, made me in the perfect image that He wants me to be. I am created *exactly* the way He wants me to be. And for that, I am thankful in ways I can't describe. And now nothing can stop me from praising my Father, my Creator.

The LORD does not look at the things people look at. People look

at the outward appearance, but the LORD *looks at the heart*
(1 Samuel 16:7).

God created mankind in his own image, in the image of God
he created them; male and female he created them (Genesis 1:27).

Matthew Responds...

So I'm flipping through the channels for a bit tonight with my
wife when I see an advertisement on the E! Network for a show called
Bridalplasty. The premise of this latest addition to the world of not-
quite-reality shows is this: Women who are engaged to be married are
brought together to compete for the chance to have a complete plas-
tic surgery makeover before the ceremony and thus to become the perfect bride for the big wedding day. Wow. So basically, now that each
woman has found her true love, someone who loves her for who she is,
she wants to change who she is right before her wedding? I cannot help
but wonder if her vows will be different from the traditional ones…
"For richer or for poorer, in sickness and in health, with your old face
or your new face…"

All joking aside, in the light of society's constant pursuit of so-called
physical perfection, my attempt to raise my two daughters with any
semblance of a positive self-image or healthy knowledge of how beautiful they really are will be an uphill climb. E.E. Cummings wrote, "To
be nobody but yourself—in a world which is doing its best, night and
day, to make you everybody else—means to fight the hardest battle
which any human being can fight; and never stop fighting."

The best way for my wife and me and any other parents to do this
is to make sure we ourselves are setting a good example by embracing
God's plan for who He created us to be, not trying to change it. When
a daughter sees her middle-aged mom trying to chase her youth, coming home after having "work" done, I wonder what type of message
this sends to her. Does she go to bed thinking, "What part of me do I
need to change?"

I don't mean to criticize—I've got just as much insecurity as the next person. If someone handed me a marker and asked me to draw a circle or an *X* on any part of my body that I didn't like, chances are I would look like a game of tic-tac-toe by the time I was finished. All people have some things they don't like about themselves. Don't let the supermodels and movie stars fool you.

To chase after perfection by the world's standards is to enter a race that no one wins. It only leads us further and further down a path of obsession with ourselves and obsession with our image. In a world of nose jobs, breast implants, and Botox, we seem to be saying, "God did the best He could, but I'll take it from here."

The Bible tells us we don't have to chase this so-called perfection. Our image needs no makeover. We were created in the image of a perfect God. "God created mankind in his own image…male and female he created them." Rick Warren writes, "God prescribed every single detail of your body. He deliberately chose your race, the color of your skin, your hair, and every other feature. He custom-made your body just the way he wanted it." David praised God for that promise: "You created my inmost being; you knit me together in my mother's womb. I praise you because I am fearfully and wonderfully made" (Psalm 139:13-14).

My good friend Mandisa was a finalist on season five of *American Idol*. While auditioning for the show, she unexpectedly faced ridicule and criticism about her weight from America's favorite nemesis, Simon Cowell. But what Simon didn't know was that Mandisa knows exactly what the definition of true beauty is. Yes, she struggles with her weight, which she has been very open about. And since her appearance on the show, she has lost more than 120 pounds. But her identity is firmly cemented in Christ. And because she was confident in who God made her to be, she was able to handle his harsh words with such grace and humility that it drove Simon to do the unimaginable—he apologized! Since then, God has continued to use Mandisa in amazing ways through her music and message to help women and young girls everywhere discover true beauty in their lives by knowing who they are in Christ.

Are you struggling with your own self-image today? Perhaps

someone in your life makes you feel inadequate or unattractive or not good enough. Or maybe you, like me, are just trying to figure out how to raise your children with the understanding that the world's definition of true beauty is all wrong. Remember that you were created in the image of a perfect God, a God who does not make mistakes. And the next time you feel tempted to join the endless chase for so-called perfection, know that your Creator is chasing after you with the promise that you are "fearfully and wonderfully made." He's the One who made you, and He wouldn't change a thing.

41

THE REASON
FOR THE WORLD

From Linda...

This Tuesday marks the first anniversary of losing our precious son, Ryan. The things that have transpired over this past year have been the most amazing things we have ever seen and more than Ryan could have imagined. He prayed to be a light for God, to make a difference, to be famous and be able to share God's love in a huge way. His prayer not to go through the motions put us all on a path we never dreamed of. Today, we gathered at his grave, and his grandfather spoke. He said, "Ryan has touched more lives in his death than he ever could have in his life." So this was Ryan's legacy, and his prayer to reach others has been answered. Our family is incomplete until we are together again someday in heaven.

"He will wipe every tear from their eyes. There will be no more death" or mourning or crying or pain (Revelation 21:4).

Blessed are those who mourn, for they will be comforted (Matthew 5:4).

Do not let your hearts be troubled...My Father's house has many rooms; if that were not so, would I have told you that I

*am going there to prepare a place for you? And if I go and pre-
pare a place for you, I will come back and take you to be with
me that you also may be where I am. You know the way to the
place where I am going* (John 14:1-4).

*Now we see only a reflection as in a mirror; then we shall see
face to face. Now I know in part; then I shall know fully, even
as I am fully known* (1 Corinthians 13:12-13).

Matthew Responds...

Ryan was an awesome 18-year-old boy from a small town in Oklahoma. His life was cut short by a tragic car accident that took place just
miles from his home. He loved his family and his friends, but most of
all, he loved God. On the night before he died, he posted this update
on his Facebook page.

> I don't wanna go through the motions
> I don't wanna go one more day
> Without Your all-consuming passion inside of me
> I don't wanna spend my whole life asking
> What if I had given everything
> Instead of going through the motions*

After the family discovered these words were from my song "The
Motions," they decided the song must be played at Ryan's memorial
service. When I heard this, I reached out to the family to let them know
they were in my prayers. They told me that at the funeral, it was clear
by the amount of people who attended and the words they spoke about
Ryan that he was a young man who lived his life to the fullest, point-
ing all who knew him in the direction of the most important part of
his life, his personal relationship with Christ. His youth pastor gave
an invitation, challenging people to make the most of every moment.
Many people did respond, making a new decision to live each day as
if it may be their last and not to settle for a life of going through the
motions. Even in this boy's death, many found a new appreciation for
life. In the past year, I have shared Ryan's story around the country in

---

the hopes of challenging all who hear that life is precious and that what we do with it matters.

Recently, I traveled to see Ryan's family in their small, rural town in Oklahoma. They invited me to join them in visiting Ryan's grave. So on an autumn afternoon, we drove a good while down a gravel road until we reached a little cemetery outside of town. The leaves had changed their color and were making their descent from their branches to the ground. The weather was turning cold, but the sun was bright and warm on our faces.

I watched Linda, Ryan's mom, brush away some dust and leaves from Ryan's gravestone, losing all track of time as we stood in silence, staring at his name carved in granite. I will never forget the experience of being side-by-side with a grieving mother, a father who has tried to be strong for his family, and an older brother who misses his best friend more than words can express. Eventually, someone spoke up, sharing a memory about Ryan. Together, we cried, laughed, and cried some more as each family member took turns telling me what made Ryan so special.

That day at Ryan's grave was a sobering reminder to me that sometimes the questions don't always find their answers so quickly. Sometimes the sorrow stays and the feelings of loss linger—unwelcome reminders that something is missing. And sometimes we could sure use a reason for this world. It was clear to me that even though a year had passed since Ryan's death, there was still so much pain in the hearts of these family members, who have been left behind to try to pick up the pieces in the wake of such tragedy.

Can you relate? Perhaps your story has been marked by its share of tragedy and loss. Maybe you have questions that can't seem to find good enough answers right now. Our questions reveal the reality that as humans, we have only been given a limited view of life. "Now I know in part; then I shall know fully." We were never designed to see the big picture the way our Creator can. He is the only One who knows the reasons why bad things happen to good people.

The last line of Linda's story really struck me. "Our family is incomplete until we are together again..." Can you feel the sense of longing in that sentence? She is acknowledging that her family is missing an important piece, but she clearly believes that someday they will be reunited once again and that their longing will be replaced by the hope of heaven fully revealed.

This is the hope we can hold on to in times of tragedy, the anchor for our souls when we are treading water in a sea of grief. This is the promise of a place called heaven; a place where every tear will be wiped away and every question will be answered. This promise makes the McAfee family long for home like they never have before. The same promise is for you to hold on to today. C.S. Lewis wrote, "If man's hunger proves he inhabits a world where food exists, my desire for Paradise is a good indication it exists." Paradise does exist. We have God's word as our evidence. And a longing for eternity is a longing that will most certainly be fulfilled.

42

I SURRENDER

From Jenny...

I lost both my parents when I was 21. They were divorced, but they died the same year. My father always loved my mother and me but was an alcoholic and chose the bottle over his family.

After the death of my parents, I did not mourn. Instead, I suppressed my feelings and began drinking to cover the pain. I married but could not physically have children. My marriage ended ten years later, and I admitted myself into a treatment center. I stayed there 30 days. I had nowhere to go, and my stepfather did not invite me in. But amazingly, an apartment came available, and I lived by myself for the first time in my life. (Yet I was not alone.) I started going to AA, which led me to God.

I always knew God but did not have a relationship with Him. A friend invited me to her church two years later, where God led me to my husband today, who is a minister. Now I have been sober 18 years and I have two beautiful stepdaughters and four grandkids. I totally surrendered my life to Jesus, and He gave me more than I ever dreamed possible. I give Him all the glory!

Take delight in the LORD, and he will give you the desires of your heart. Commit your way to the LORD; trust in him and he will do this: He will make your righteous reward shine like the dawn (Psalm 37:5-6).

Submit yourselves, then, to God. Resist the devil, and he will flee from you. Come near to God and he will come near to you…Humble yourselves before the Lord, and he will lift you up (James 4:7-8,10).

Angela Responds…

Surrender is one of the great ironies of God. When we surrender our lives to God, we give up. We give up our own control. We concede our rebellious hearts. We lay down our sin. In effect, we are like the battle weary who raise the white flag and yell toward heaven, "Take me captive; I'm yours."

But surrendering to God is altogether different from surrendering to an enemy. In movies, we see defeated warriors being hauled off in chains, locked in cells, and given barely enough rations to survive. The newly surrendered prisoners might be shamed or tortured as a part of their punishment. That kind of surrender means all freedom is lost. I think that sometimes we have believed surrendering to God is the same. Chains. Shame. All freedom is gone.

But surrendering to God is a beautiful irony because when you give your life completely to Him, when you place yourself inside the strong embrace of His love, when you turn your back on where you have been and look to God for every next step, only then are you free. For some, the word *surrender* means to stop living. But in fact—oh, hallelujah!—because of Jesus, just the opposite is true. When you surrender to God, that's exactly when you begin to live! Even better, you don't live aimlessly; you live with the purpose that God has planned for you.

Jenny's story is similar to so many of our stories. Many of us could place ourselves along the same path her life has taken. Sad circumstances. Exposure to poor choices. Choosing a way to mask the pain. A broken relationship. Complete and total emptiness. Loneliness. Finally, all that's left are you and your consequences before God. But that is exactly where Jenny made the choice that transformed her life. She surrendered herself fully to God. Remember? She said she had always known God, but a day finally came when she gave every decision to Him. Surrender.

I don't know where you find yourself on this path today, but I can tell you with complete assurance that if you have not surrendered your life to Christ, you will continue to walk your version of a broken life. Only God has the power to transform.

Right now I am praying for you as you read this. Do you want to live in freedom, fully loved and eternally cared for? Do you want to be different? Act better? Choose wisely? Live in blessing? If so, I pray that today you'll give up. That you'll stop living for yourself and surrender your life to the One who gives new life.

And then I'm praying that when you sit down to write the story of your life, your words will sound a lot like Jenny's: "He gave me more than I ever dreamed possible!"

43

THE POWER OF FORGIVENESS

From Renee...

I never understood why God would ask Abraham to sacrifice Issac, the son he waited so long to have. I also always hoped He would never require such a sacrifice of me. The love a parent has for a child is like no other. God blessed me with three daughters (the last two are identical twins). I love my children with all my heart and could never imagine living without one of them.

I now have a mission I did not choose: DUI presentations.

On May 11, 2002, a 24-year-old drunk driver named Eric killed one of my twins, Meagan, and one of her friends, Lisa. Both girls were 20 years old. This was devastating for all three families involved and for countless friends who mourned the loss of these precious girls. But this is also a story of forgiveness and healing. My family and Lisa's family chose to forgive Eric. We even appealed to have his 22-year prison sentence reduced to 11 years.

Since March 29, 2004 I have traveled all over the country, telling this story to thousands of people, mostly teenagers. I always talk about forgiveness because we have learned how powerful it is for everyone. Eric told me he has his eternal salvation because of Meagan and Lisa. I show a video of him in my presentations and will soon have him standing with me, a living, breathing example of the dangers of drunk driving and the power of forgiveness.

Blessed are the merciful, for they will be shown mercy (Matthew 5:7).

Forgive us our debts, as we have forgiven our debtors (Matthew 6:12).

Be kind and compassionate to one another, forgiving each other, just as in Christ God forgave you (Ephesians 4:32).

You have heard that it was said, "Love your neighbor and hate your enemy." But I tell you, love your enemies and pray for those who persecute you, that you may be children of your Father in heaven (Matthew 5:43-45).

Matthew Responds...

I cannot think of a more vivid, modern-day example of the power of forgiveness than Renee's story. No parent should ever have to face what she did. Being a parent myself, the thought of receiving a phone call with the horrifying news that my child's life had been taken is too horrible to wrap my mind around. And yet that has become Renee's reality. A drunk driver who never should have been behind the wheel of a car that night senselessly killed her beloved daughter.

Few would blame Renee for any resentment or even hatred she may harbor toward this criminal, who stole her daughter away from her. Even the most gracious seem to have their limits. Many would say she has a right to hold a grudge. After all, the young man was found guilty by a judge and jury. Even the law is on Renee's side. Yet somehow, she has found it in her heart to extend the hope of forgiveness to this guilty man who took the life of her daughter, and both of their lives changed as a result.

If you are anything like me, reading Renee's story may have left you a bit conflicted. One of my first thoughts was, "I'm not sure I could do the same." I thought about how much I love my daughters. My flesh tells me that if someone took them away from me the way Eric took Megan and Lisa, forgiveness would be impossible. And while I am being honest, I should probably confess that I have a hard enough time forgiving the person who cut in front of me at the grocery checkout, or even my wife when we find ourselves at odds, let alone someone who has done irreparable harm to myself or my family.

Yes, unfortunately, holding a grudge is something I do quite well. How about you? Is there someone in your life who wronged you? Maybe a relationship that has been severed because a lie was told or trust betrayed? Or perhaps you relate to Renee's story. Having been wronged by a complete stranger, you hold on to a deep resentment that you carry with you every moment of every day. Maybe someone has stolen away something or someone so precious to you that you can never get back. Big or small, forgiveness can be a seemingly impossible bridge to cross.

Philip Yancey, in his book *What's So Amazing About Grace?*, describes forgiveness as an unnatural act. I could not agree more.

> I never find forgiveness easy, and rarely do I find it completely satisfying. Nagging injustices remain, and the wounds still cause pain. I have to approach God again and again, yielding to him the residue of what I thought I had committed to him long ago. I do so because the Gospels make clear the connection: God forgives my debts as I forgive my debtors.*

Forgiveness makes little sense when we are the ones being asked to forgive. It goes against everything we feel inside when we are the wronged party. And being the flawed humans we are, we do have our limits. However, when we are the ones in need of forgiveness, well, isn't that quite a different story?

C.S. Lewis wrote, "To be a Christian means to forgive the inexcusable, because God has forgiven the inexcusable in you." Let us always

---

* Philip Yancey, *What's So Amazing About Grace?* (Grand Rapids: Zondervan, 2002), 93.

be mindful of our own deep and endless need for forgiveness, and grateful for the limitless forgiveness that is extended to us through Christ's sacrifice on the cross. Let us be grateful that He did not wait for us to make the first move. "God demonstrates his own love for us in this; while we were still sinners, Christ died for us" (Romans 5:8). He initiated forgiveness of our sins, and in doing so, released its healing power into the lives of all who accept.

By forgiving Eric, Renee has made a choice to humbly follow the example Christ set for us, and God has used her step of faith to release healing into both of their lives, leading Eric to find his own personal freedom in Christ. And what is it about Renee that would allow her to see her perpetrator through eyes of grace and not anger? When our hearts and souls are awakened to the need of forgiveness in our own lives, we will be more inclined to see our enemies through eyes of compassion. Jesus laying down His own life for our sins is the truest example of how we should forgive others. And the reward of forgiveness is great.

> Forgiveness is a rebirth of hope, a reorganization of thought, and a reconstruction of dreams. Once forgiving begins, dreams can be rebuilt. When forgiving is complete, meaning has been extracted from the worst of experiences and used to create a new set of moral rules and a new interpretation of life's events.[*]

This is the reward Renee has been blessed to discover. Yes, she still hurts. Yes, she still misses her daughter. But forgiveness can bring hope to our hopeless tragedies and freedom from the burden of resentment. Lewis B. Smedes wrote, "When we genuinely forgive, we set a prisoner free and then discover that the prisoner we set free was us."[†] Set yourself free. Carry Renee's story with you this week and ask God to help you follow His example of forgiveness toward someone who has wronged you.

---

[*] Beverly Flanigan, *Forgiving the Unforgivable* (Hoboken, NJ: Wiley, 1994), 29.

[†] Lewis B. Smedes, *Shame and Grace* (New York: HarperOne, 1994), 141.

44

SET FREE

From Tim...

I was 33 years old, and Christ was knocking at the door. I had a hard life growing up and had become very self-reliant. But it wasn't enough anymore. I had married the girl of my dreams, we had two wonderful kids...but we were having financial troubles. My self-reliance couldn't save the day.

I finally realized where to turn, but it seemed I might be too late. I had said no to Christ so many times, and it seemed a giant chain was attached to my ankle. Every time I said no, another link was added to the chain. Whenever I wanted to respond to the invitation in our small-town church, the chain held me back. I would go home and get in the closet and weep.

Finally I decided to give it one more try. I bypassed my usual place in the back row of the church and went to a pew closer to the front. As soon as the invitation was out of the pastor's mouth, I shot forward as if out of a cannon.

My life has never been the same, and Jesus and I are twice the man I was by myself. My wife and I have now been married 27 years, and the kids are grown. Whenever I get the opportunity to witness to others, I usually end by asking, "Aren't you tired of dragging that chain around?"

Scripture has locked up everything under the control of sin (Galatians 3:22).

I see another law at work in me, waging war against the law of my mind and making me a prisoner of the law of sin at work within me. What a wretched man I am! Who will rescue me from this body that is subject to death? Thanks be to God, who delivers me through Jesus Christ our Lord! (Romans 7:23-25).

The Spirit of the Sovereign LORD is on me, because the LORD has anointed me to proclaim good news to the poor. He has sent me to bind up the brokenhearted, to proclaim freedom for the captives and release from darkness for the prisoners (Isaiah 61:1-2).

It is for freedom that Christ has set us free. Stand firm, then, and do not let yourselves be burdened again by a yoke of slavery (Galatians 5:1).

Angela Responds...

A life in chains. A prisoner to sin. Imagine that person, a person meant to live and dance and love, now shackled to a wall, subjected to darkness. Lonely and hungry. The Bible uses the image of a prisoner in chains so we can imagine what it feels like to live a life without Jesus Christ.

Maybe today that prisoner is you. Even though you never intended it to happen, maybe you feel as if you are chained to a wall, and you long to be free. Chained to old habits. Sin patterns. Poor communication and difficult relationships. The consequences of your choices. Maybe the chains are feeling heavier and heavier, and life feels more like a prison than a place of freedom.

Do you know that not one person can avoid the shackles of sin? Every one of us has been a slave. Truly. The Bible says that all have sinned and that no one gets a pass to avoid its chains. Each one of us is born with a frustrating and ugly sin nature. In the book of Romans, the apostle Paul is so angered by his sin, he shouts to his readers, "What a wretched man I am!" Maybe you sometimes feel like shouting the same thing.

Then Paul asks, "Who will rescue me from this body that is subject to death?" I love that in this passage, he immediately answers his own question. As soon as he asks, his spirit responds, "Thanks be to God, who delivers me through Jesus Christ our Lord!" Jesus is the answer. Jesus is the only way to be freed from the chains of our sin.

Do you long to be free? The entire Bible, every story and every weighty theological truth, points to this one thing: Jesus Christ came, lived, and died so you and I could be free. Tim will never forget the day he asked Jesus to rescue him from the chains of his sin. I love what he says: "Jesus and I are twice the man I was by myself."

Here's what to do if today is the day you choose freedom over the chains:

- Wherever you are, you can talk to God right now. It's called prayer, but really, it's just talking to the One who loves you so.
- In your own words, tell God that you believe He sent His Son, Jesus, to rescue you.
- Ask God to forgive you of your sins. He promises to forgive when you ask.
- Ask God to teach you how to become a follower of Jesus. Let Him teach you how to live your life in His promised freedom.

There are no tricks with God. He doesn't try to make it hard. We are the ones who have made our lives complicated, but God offers a freedom that is simple. Follow Jesus. Give your life to Him. Let His forgiveness make you clean.

I am praying for you as I write. I'm praying that Tim's story and the truths of Scripture will be the words that set you free. I'm praying today would be the day your chains are broken. I'm praying no matter how many years you have lived in chains, the desire to be free would be greater than any other temptation. Maybe you have already realized that you are powerless to break your chains. But my friend, God is able.

May you choose Christ today!

Let the chains fall and the freedom begin!

45

BE IMITATORS

From Becky...

I was saved when I was nine, but then I went through a rebellion against everything I knew to be true. My father, a deacon and a very godly man, was my rock throughout it all. I was a single mother of two small children, and he was their male role model also. My world crumbled when we learned my dad, my rock, had inoperable brain cancer.

When he was debilitated and too weak to feed himself or care for his most basic needs, he said to me, "God is so good to me."

I was so angry, both at him and at God, and I retorted, "What are you talking about? Look at you! You can't feed yourself, you can't go to the bathroom by yourself, you are dying! If that is how good God is, leave me out of it!"

He just grasped my hand and said, "Cancer is painful, but I don't have any pain at all."

For months I had railed against God, screaming and crying out, begging Him not to take my father. After Dad died, I realized just how much God loved me. Just as Jesus sacrificed His life for us, I felt my dad had sacrificed his life so I could learn to depend upon God instead of him. What a great imitator of Christ my father was!

This has made it even easier for me to now cry out, "Abba, Father!" with love and joy.

Follow God's example, therefore, as dearly loved children and walk in the way of love, just as Christ loved us and gave himself up for us as a fragrant offering and sacrifice to God (Ephesians 5:1).

In your relationships with one another, have the same mindset as Christ Jesus (Philippians 2:5).

Angela Responds…

The story of Becky's dad challenges me deeply. When others look at us, do they see people who are imitating Christ or people who are focused mostly on themselves? How I pray that I would imitate the beauty of Christ's life the way Becky's dad did. If I say that I belong to Christ, oh, how I pray that I can live the way He lived. Give the way He gave. And if my turn comes, may I suffer the way He suffered—with grace.

To be an imitator of Jesus Christ is to live by the overarching principles that Jesus taught and modeled in the New Testament. Becoming an imitator doesn't mean wearing the same clothes or eating the same things or living in the same place. To imitate Christ is to assimilate the truths of the Bible into your life, with your personality woven thoroughly through your calling. To imitate Christ means that in your everyday life, wherever you are, you are consciously choosing to become more and more like Jesus and less and less like the self-focused person you could have been.

Modeling the attitude of Christ will affect every area of your life—your relationships, decisions, service, stress levels…you name it. To imitate Christ means that the power of the Holy Spirit is radically transforming who you are, inside and out. But just how does one begin to grow in this practice? How do you just turn over a new leaf and start acting like Jesus? I think for most of us, it's a journey.

In my own life, God seems to prompt me about what's next. I want the whole attitude of Christ all at once, but in my humanity, I seem to be a slow learner, and one thing at a time is much more practical. When I wanted to become more like Christ in the area of prayer, I learned to incorporate the mind-set of prayer into different places during my day. For a season, I focused on learning everything I could about prayer. In much the same way, right now, God has me working through an area of forgiveness. I long to have the compassionate heart of Christ and not the selfish, painful heart I have known. I am learning.

How about you? Becky's dad didn't just become an imitator of Christ in his sickness. That kind of soul change came as he walked a faithful journey of learning from Christ, growing in His grace, and becoming more like Him all the years of his life.

What if you bowed your head in the next few minutes and just said these few things to God?

> I do want to look like Jesus.
> But I know I am not strong enough to instantly
>   become all I want to be.
> Will You teach me? Will You show me where to
>   start today?
> I want to be faithful.
> I long for everyone I encounter to see Jesus in me.
> Amen.

Here is what I know about God: He has never asked for perfection from us. He has always looked for willingness. God can mightily transform a willing heart. May we become imitators of Christ—for all to see!

46

TWO HOUSES

From Joly...

I am a 15-year-old girl who seemed to have the perfect life—until everything changed in the blink of an eye. My father left us after hurting me and my family a lot. I didn't understand how he could do this. At one point, I asked God to take my life away if it would bring my family back together.

I was very angry, frustrated, and hurt, so my mom told me to take my feelings and problems to God in prayer. I had been a Christian before that, but until the moment I went to God in my pain, I had never truly experienced an intimate relationship with my Savior. Every day He sent me comfort through the Bible.

My favorite verse is Romans 8:28: "We know that in all things God works for the good of those who love him, who have been called according to his purpose." How *true* is that verse! I am so grateful that God used this to happen in my life, to bring me closer to Him! Now, instead of being angry with my father, I have forgiven him and pray for him every day.

Yes, at times I'm scared because I do not know what tomorrow holds, but I do know that God holds tomorrow! That's such a comforting thought. Now I want to help other kids who are going through the same pain as me. I want to tell them they have an ever-loving Father in heaven who will never leave or forsake them.

If they will only lay their troubles at His feet, He will sustain them (Psalm 55:22).

Look at the birds of the air; they do not sow or reap or store away in barns, and yet your heavenly Father feeds them. Are you not much more valuable than they? (Matthew 6:26).

A father to the fatherless…is God in his holy dwelling (Psalm 68:5).

Matthew Responds…

Sadly, way too many people know exactly what it is like to go through what Joly has experienced in her life recently. The divorce rate in America is more than 50 percent. This means that one in two couples will break up. Every 30 seconds there is a divorce in America. And many of these broken homes are filled with children who are left to try to deal with a new reality, a reality where nothing looks the way it once did. Read the lyrics to a song called "Two Houses" that I wrote after reading Joly's story.

Two Houses

Mom found her a new place to live
Dad found him a new girlfriend
Looks like everybody's moving on
And its "Hey, look on the bright side, kid
Now you got two Christmases"
And it's every other weekend from now on

But all I want is the way it was…
When love would always last forever
And family stayed together
Back to the day before two houses
When they held my hand and I was little
Before I got caught in the middle
Somewhere in between two houses
'Cause these two houses sure don't feel like home*

After writing the song, I read those lyrics to my wife. When I was finished I looked up to see tears streaming down her face. "That's true," she said. "The words you wrote, they are true." She would know. Emily's parents divorced when she was just four years old, and I have learned through her how deeply divorce can wound a child.

People say kids are tough. They're resilient. They can make it through anything. That may be true at times, but it can also be used as a rationalization so the truth won't hurt as badly. The *real* truth is this: When children see their parents break up, they are forced to find new definitions for words like *love, trust, truth,* and *commitment.* Innocence falls victim to the harsh reality that things don't always stay the same.

Can you relate? Perhaps you know how it feels to feel abandoned by someone you love. If so, Joly would like you to know that just like her, you have never really been alone. She wants you to discover the same comforting hope she found. As she turned to God in her loneliest moments, she felt the arms of her heavenly Father holding her and her broken heart. Even though her "perfect life" did not look so perfect after all, she is now looking to the only real source that can help her begin to redefine these words:

> *Love.* "He is good; His love endures forever" (2 Chronicles 5:13).
>
> *Trust.* "In God I trust and am not afraid" (Psalm 56:4).
>
> *Truth.* "I am the way and the truth and the life" (John 14:6).
>
> *Commitment.* "Never will I leave you; never will I forsake you" (Hebrews 13:5).

Take great comfort in these Scriptures today and remember that you have never been alone and will never be. Throughout each and every single page of the story of your life, a constant companion is accompanying you. Regardless of who has walked out on you, disappointed you, or let you down in your life, there is One who will never leave—Jesus.

47

WORLD CHANGER

From Jon...

I am a college student in Philadelphia, and I was changed by the Lord when I was in high school. My story is about change.

I gave my life to Jesus after a conference in Texas, and ever since then it's been a journey. The transition from high school to college has been the biggest test I have faced. I absolutely hated my freshmen year of college. I had no idea why the Lord would uproot me from my comfort zone of family and friends and place me in urban Philadelphia. It was a fast downhill spiral of tears and depression. I was mad at God. This change was destroying me.

However, this changed when the Lord led me to serve the city of Philadelphia during a spring break. I experienced the brokenness, the crime, and the love of the people, and I established a true heart for the city. Since that experience, the Lord has been revealing to me why He called me out of my comfort zone and why He wanted my world to change. I have a heart for urban areas now. I find myself leading others to live like Jesus by loving the outcast, the strangers, and the forgotten people in the city. I am blessed by a God who provides me with opportunities to lead others through changes in their lives, and am loved by a God who will always help me face the next chapter of life.

> *Speak up for those who cannot speak for themselves, for the*
> *rights of all who are destitute. Speak up and judge fairly;*
> *defend the rights of the poor and needy* (Proverbs 31:8-9).

> *If anyone has material possessions and sees his brother or sister*
> *in need but has no pity on them, how can the love of God be in*
> *that person? Dear children, let us not love with words or speech*
> *but with actions and in truth* (1 John 3:17-18).

Angela Responds...

God changes us so that through us, He can change the world!

When you and I become followers of Jesus, the Holy Spirit begins to do an amazing thing—He transforms our very natures. With every new experience, the people we used to be are being molded into the image of Christ. The whole idea is that in this life, we would look more and more like Jesus and less and less like the old, all-about-me people we have been. God wants to use us, the changed ones, to be His hands and feet to the rest of this world.

I don't know about you, but I have found that my personality is naturally resistant to change. I like things the way they have always been. I like to drive the same route home, use the same meat loaf recipe I have followed for years, plant the same flowers in my yard, and sit in the same seat at church on Sundays. I am naturally inclined to stay put. To go with what I know. To coast on my generally consistent sameness.

But God is not content for me to stay the same. He keeps calling me up and out. Up toward greater spiritual maturity. Out toward this world and His purposes. I truly want to be a passionate follower of Christ, but the part about changing is the place where I can stumble or hesitate. The transition from where I have been to where God is taking me is the place where it hurts sometimes. That's where I can feel a loneliness, where questions crop up and I wonder what in the world God is doing.

I love that Jon tells us that changing was hard for him until he began to understand what God wanted to do with a changed man. God wanted to use him! I think God wants to use you and me too. And for both of us, a little change may be required.

Maybe God is softening your heart so you can begin to feel the hurts of others. Maybe He is changing your city so you can see the hurting people you may have missed in your familiar town. Maybe He is allowing a season of less so you will never forget how it feels when you have more. Maybe He is slowing you down so you don't run past the needy. Every change is like a fine-tuning of the soul. If we let Him, God will use every change to shape us for kingdom work.

I'm praying that God will do for us what He did for Jon—give us eyes to see, hearts to feel, and hands to obey. I want to pray this prayer more often:

> God, change me so that You can use me to change this world. I want to be a world changer. I am embarrassed that I have long ignored the needs around me. Please forgive me and make me aware. Make me different. Make me an instrument of Your love.

Maybe the next time we feel uncomfortable about a change in our lives, instead of feeling sorry for ourselves or recounting our old lives, we will turn our eyes toward God and ask, "Are You up to something? Something that is about Your kingdom and not really about me?"

And then maybe our faith will kick in and our trust will lead to peace, and from the bottom of our hearts we will shout like we mean it: "*Use me!*"

48

WHAT A THANK-YOU CAN DO

From Candy...

I was a small-town country girl raised in a coal-mining town in Pennsylvania. At the age of 18, I moved by myself to Washington, DC. I was in DC for a little more than a year and messed up my life with guys, alcohol, and drugs. But then one day while I was hitch-hiking, God saved me. I prayed the sinner's prayer with a person who picked me up, not even really understanding what I was doing. But the Holy Spirit came to me, and I could feel Him saying, "You are a new creation now."

That day I started a change in my life. I started praying, reading my Bible, and going to church three times a week. It's been almost 38 years since that day. "Thank You, God, for saving me and transforming me. Thank You for rescuing this alcoholic. Thank You for redeeming this drug addict. Thank You for forgiving this prostitute. Thank You for giving me a wonderful husband of 32 years and keeping my life on a straight course. Thank You! Thank You! Lord, thank You!"

Give thanks to the LORD, for he is good; his love endures forever (Psalm 107:1).

Give thanks in all circumstances; for this is God's will for you in Christ Jesus (1 Thessalonians 5:18).

Do not be anxious about anything, but in every situation, by prayer and petition, with thanksgiving, present your requests to God. And the peace of God, which transcends all understanding, will guard your hearts and your minds in Christ Jesus (Philippians 4:6-7).

Matthew Responds...

My youngest daughter, Delaney, is becoming quite the little talker. She's not quite two years old and attempts to carry on conversations with us all day long. Of course, we only understand every third word or so (just as if we were listening to Ozzy Osbourne). But it sure seems to make sense to her.

One phrase comes through crystal clear, however: "Thank you." Well, the *T*s and *Y*s sound a lot like *D*s, so it comes out more like "Dank dou." But for Delaney, "Thank you" seems to be a response for all occasions.

"Delaney, did you have a nice nap?"

"Dank dou."

"No, no, Delaney—no climbing into the dishwasher."

"Dank dou."

"Oh, Delaney, that is one stinky diaper!"

"Dank dou."

Crazy, I know, but perhaps Delaney is on the right track by making "thank you" her go-to response. Judging from Candy's story, I bet she would agree. Her story jumped out at me among the thousands I read because of the sheer number of times she wrote the words *thank You*. One minute she was telling me her story, where she's from and the poor choices she made, and the next minute she breaks into a prayer of thanksgiving to God.

I could just picture sitting down with Candy and hearing the story of her life in person. I picture her eyes going back and forth from me to heaven every time she says another "Thank You!" Thornton Wilder wrote, "We can only be said to be alive in those moments when our hearts are conscious of our treasures." One glance at Candy's story, and you can tell that she is living her life conscious of her treasures, and her heart is filled with gratitude.

Is yours? Are you quick to give thanks or to complain? I know what my answer is to that question. Hands down, I complain first. If there were an Olympics for complainers, I would be standing on the center podium accepting the gold medal. I'm the kind of person who can have nine out of ten things in my life going amazingly well, and guess what I will choose to focus on? Without fail, my mind focuses solely on the one thing that is still not quite where I think it should be to be deemed worthy of my gratitude. If you can relate, then we've got to try a different approach.

Henry Ward Beecher wrote, "The unthankful heart…discovers no mercies; but let the thankful heart sweep through the day and, as the magnet finds the iron, so it will find, in every hour, some heavenly blessings!" An unthankful heart is at risk of missing out on all that a thankful heart has to offer to your story.

Now, thanking God for the good things is usually not that much of a challenge. Thanking God for the negative circumstances is much less natural. Yet the Bible does not say we should give thanks only in the good times. Instead it challenges us, "Give thanks in *all* circumstances." How can that be? Thankful for my blessings? Piece of cake. Thankful for my problems? Houston, we have a problem.

Why is it so important to be thankful for our problems? Because when we thank God, our focus shifts from the problem to the solution. To thank God for our problems is to trust that He is big enough to come through for us in any and every circumstance. And the only way to achieve this grateful attitude is to spend time daily in the presence of God. There, in the light of His presence, our problems and circumstances slowly drift into the background as heavenly peace gently alters our perspective.

Practice thankfulness today. Start your quiet time in God's presence by lifting up gratitude to His great name.

- *Thank Him for all He has done.* "[I will] daily add praise to praise. I'll write the book on your righteousness, talk

up your salvation the livelong day, never run out of good
things to write or say" (Psalm 71:14-15 MSG).

- *Thank Him for all He is going to do.* "Thanks be to God!
  He gives us the victory through our Lord Jesus Christ"
  (1 Corinthians 15:57).

- *Thank Him for His saving grace.* "It is by grace you have
  been saved" (Ephesians 2:8).

- *Thank Him for being God.* "If God is for us, who can be
  against us?" (Romans 8:31).

Thank Him for stories like Candy's that remind us that we too have
so much to be thankful for. Thank Him for bringing meaning and
joy to every chapter in the story of your life. Practice this attitude of
thanks in His presence today, and you will discover like Delaney did
that "thank you" is indeed a response for all occasions.

49

GOD'S PURPOSE OR YOUR PLANS?

From Emily...

I had everything figured out and was pursuing my dream job in the United States Secret Service. I had only one more test left before heading into training.

Before beginning my new job, I decided to take one last short-term mission trip. During those ten days in Ghana, God broke my heart for ministry. I couldn't see myself working for 50 weeks a year just so I could go on a short-term mission trip for two weeks. All my life, I had said there was no way I was going to grow up and be a missionary like my parents. *No way!* But God softened my heart. He broke down my stubbornness and showed me His will for my life.

At the end of this month, instead of pursuing my dream job and going to officer training, I have a new dream and will be heading to candidate orientation for a mission agency working in Africa. I am scared of what this means for my life, but I'm so excited to be living in the center of God's will!

Therefore go and make disciples of all nations, baptizing them in the name of the Father and of the Son and of the Holy Spirit,

*and teaching them to obey everything I have commanded you.
And surely I am with you always, to the very end of the age*
(Matthew 28:19-20).

*You are the salt of the earth…You are the light of the world.
A town built on a hill cannot be hidden* (Matthew 5:13-15).

Matthew Responds…

I grew up in the front-row pew. My dad has been a preacher longer than I have been alive, and every Sunday, like clockwork, my brothers and I made our way to the front of the church and sat with Mom while Dad preached. My father has always had a heart for missions, and as a result, our church has supported the work of many missionaries stationed around the world. On special Sundays, missionaries we supported visited and spoke at our church, telling wonderful stories of their work for the kingdom in exotic, faraway places.

My brothers and I loved these Sundays (mostly because we knew we would get to go out to lunch at Chili's with the missionaries after the service). I remember feeling two vastly different emotions while listening to these extreme stories from servants who gave up everything to spread the gospel overseas: fascination and fear. I was fascinated by the notion of someone leaving all the comforts we've come to know and love, yet I was fearful that God might call *me* to do the same!

Somewhere along the line, I got it in my head that God would call me to do the one thing I did not want to do, as if He took delight in making me miserable. So I remember devising a plan to trick God. I thought, "If I tell God I'm willing to be a missionary to Africa, He won't send me." For some reason, I thought I needed to (and could) outwit God, so I contrived this prayer: "God, I will go to Africa. If You want me to go, I'll go." I hoped that my little scheme would work, that God would believe I was willing to go to the ends of the earth and therefore allow me to stay home.

Crazy, right? Of course, now that I am older I have come to see that (1) there is no fooling God. He knows our thoughts and sees the true condition of our hearts. And (2) even though pursuing God's plan for our lives may require that we venture out beyond the safety of a comfortable life, ultimately the single best place any of us could find ourselves is in the center of His plan for our lives, whether in Somalia or the suburbs.

Have you ever thought that maybe the story of *your* life could have a global impact?

Or maybe you can relate to my childhood prayer. Maybe you want to believe you would be willing to go wherever God calls you, but deep down you are not sure you could part with the comforts of the American dream.

I used to think that only a few choice followers of Christ were called to missions. For example, my cousin feels called to be a missionary in Africa. I feel called to work here in the States. But I have begun to realize that our "callings" may not be so cut-and-dried after all and that God's plan for each of our stories is to reach the world. In his book *Radical*, David Platt describes an eye-opening moment of clarity while standing on top of a mountain overlooking millions upon millions of lost people in India.

> And then it hit me. The overwhelming majority of these people had never even heard the gospel. They offer religious sacrifices day in and day out because no one has told them that, in Christ, the final sacrifice has already been offered on their behalf. As a result they live without Christ, and if nothing changes, they will die without him as well.
>
> As I stood on that mountain, God gripped my heart and flooded my mind with two resounding words: "Wake up." Wake up and realize that there are infinitely more important things in your life than football and a 401(k). Wake up and realize there are real battles to be fought, so different from the superficial, meaningless "battles" you focus on. Wake up to the countless multitudes who are currently destined for a Christless eternity.*

---

* David Platt, *Radical: Taking Back Your Faith from the American Dream* (Colorado Springs: Multnomah Books, 2009), 14.

It sounds idealistic, I know. Impact the world. But doesn't it also sound biblical? God has created us to accomplish a radically global, supremely God-exalting purpose with our lives. The formal definition of *impact* is "a forcible contact between two things," and God has designed our lives for a collision course with the world.

Too often, many of us Christians simply ignore God's true calling for our lives because we simply cannot bear the thought of parting with a comfortable lifestyle. Well, Emily's life now looks different from what she thought it would. She opened her heart and allowed God to lead her down a path that diverged from the so-called American dream. I love the last sentence of her story: "I'm scared of what this means for my life, but I am so excited to be in the center of God's will!" Today, ask God how He wants to use your life to reach the world.

Perhaps you could begin to support a missions organization financially or through prayer. Have you ever taken a missions trip to another part of the world? Pray about taking some steps like these. Rest assured that God does not delight in making you miserable. "I have come that they may have life, and have it to the full" (John 10:10). Ask God to help you simply act in obedience when He places a certain cause or even a country on your heart. And then, like Emily, take a step of faith. Let her story inspire you today to choose sacrifice instead of safety, excitement instead of excuses, and God's purpose instead of your plans. You will be amazed to see the way your story will impact the world.

50

THE BIGGEST
LITTLE STORY EVER

From Sheila...

I have no story. Nothing of interest. I am not a person of influence. I wasn't saved in jail. I have no unhealthy addictions. I was never abused or homeless. I've never been to war or recognized as a hero. I don't have incredible strength or fame. I don't have an illness that drew me close to the Lord in desperation. I've not had to go through the unimaginable pain of losing a child or spouse.

I was saved in church when I was ten years old. There was no dramatic lifestyle change that came with my salvation. I was ten! So when I sit down to write my testimony, Satan whispers in my ear, "Your life isn't interesting. You have nothing to say."

Now I am 30 years old, and all my life I have felt like I have no testimony. I am just a working mom. A wife. I may never do anything that this world classifies as big, and yet I know that I am not insignificant. But what's my story? How does a woman like me make a difference for Christ? I pray that it's in the little things. I hope it's seen in the lives of my kids when they sing along to Christian radio. I pray it's in the day they surrendered their lives to Christ. I pray that the little ways I try to show God's love make a difference.

Without Him I would truly have no story, but more importantly, no future!

> *To him who is able to keep you from stumbling and to present you before his glorious presence without fault and with great joy—to the only God our Savior be glory, majesty, power and authority, through Jesus Christ our Lord, before all ages, now and forevermore! Amen* (Jude 24).

> *Jesus replied: "'Love the Lord your God with all your heart and with all your soul and with all your mind.' This is the first and greatest commandment"* (Matthew 22:37-38).

Angela Responds...

If Jesus were to write Sheila a personal letter, I wonder if it might look something like this.

> Dear Sheila,
>
> I wish you could see Me smiling. I wish you could hear Me singing love songs over you. Oh, my sweet beloved, if there was ever a woman with a story, it's you. It's just that the story is not as much about you as it is about Me. Do you know how blessed I am by your life? Do you know how pleased I am that for 20 years, you have loved Me with all of your heart, soul, and mind?
>
> Here is the story I see in you. A little girl of ten says she want to follow Me, and she means it. Then she lives every day with Me—trusting Me, learning to be faithful, and running to Me with her pain. She grows in wisdom and stature. She receives her discipline and learns from it. She realizes her need of forgiveness and asks Me for it. Oh, Sheila, your story is the story of Me in your life. Your story is the story of My protection, My provision, My guidance. I gave and you obeyed. There is the glory, My precious child.

I am glorified in your consistent faith. I am glorified when you love your family. I am glorified by each little choice you make that points to Me.

And you are right—Satan is the deceiver. He whispers to the faithful, "You are not enough. Your life is not significant. Living a gentle and good life is not a big deal." But Sheila, you are such a big deal in heaven. I see the way you love, and I'm so proud of you. I stand in your house, watching the way you serve with humility. You imitate Me, and there is no greater compliment. You glorify Me with your purity and your grace.

Oh, how I wish more of My followers had such a big little story. We could change the world, one family at a time, one community at a time with more Sheilas living powerfully faithful lives. No flashy testimony suits Me just fine. I beam over your faithfulness.

My sweet girl, I want you to be encouraged. I want you to keep living the big story of My Spirit in you. Keep being faithful in the small things. That means more to Me than this world may ever realize. Keep looking to Me for wisdom and grace. Do you hear Me shouting for joy? I *love* your story because every day, your story points to Me.

And so my daughter, grow in the knowledge of My love for you. Keep living your beautiful, big story for My glory…so the world may know.

> I am forever,
> Jesus, your Savior and Friend

51

DEAR ANONYMOUS

From Anonymous...

Well, I've fought writing this since I read about it on your twitter page, but a part of me needs to finally speak out about my story. First of all, I'm also a songwriter, so I really believe in the power of music. If I inspired a song for you then maybe it would help me. Anyway, I'm 20 years old, and since I was 12 years old I've had a dream to be a recording artist. I've been singing in church my whole life, and I've always known that God has called me to do great things.

I've grown up in a Christian home and always known right from wrong, but for as long as I can remember, I've dealt with homosexuality. I've never acted on this, but I deal with it on a daily basis. I don't understand why, but my whole life I've had that problem.

Every day is a fight, and I tell myself that God has *big* plans for me and that Satan won't relent because he knows what God has in store for me and he's trying to stop it. I sit and cry because I try *so* hard to live a life pleasing to God, and this hasn't gone away. I didn't ask to deal with this, and it certainly isn't easy to deal with. It's something I have never shared with anyone until now. It's something I'm ashamed of—I hate myself for it most days.

I just don't know what to do or how to fix this. If it weren't for my dreams I wouldn't have the strength to keep on. I feel like I hide and that it's not okay to be myself. I want to know what freedom feels like; I want to know how it feels to be able to live my life without the weight of the world crashing down on me. I want this to go away, but I'm too ashamed to talk about it with anyone. This is keeping me from all I've wanted, and I hate the twisted view of love that I have.

If anyone is in Christ, the new creation has come (2 Corinthians 5:17).

No temptation has overtaken you except what is common to man. And God is faithful; he will not let you be tempted beyond what you can bear. But when you are tempted, he will also provide a way out so that you can endure it (1 Corinthians 10:13).

Angela Responds...

This is the letter I would send to this dear person if I could.

Dear Anonymous,

I may never meet you, but I want you to know one thing up front, though our stories, our sin, and our weakness may be different, we both need Jesus the same. I am so very aware that you and I meet at the foot of the cross, both kneeling before the grace of God, asking Jesus to save us from this fallen world and the way it torments our souls. I also want you to know that I am sorry for all the pain you suffer and the burdens you carry. I am so very glad you wrote your story. My heart tells me that what you have written speaks for thousands of others who also suffer in silence.

I have been praying for you for weeks now, wondering how I might write to you from the truth of Scripture. Asking God what His guidance would be. My struggles are not the same as yours, but nonetheless, I believe I am supposed to offer to you what has been given to me—compassion. I also want you to know that I am new to this kind of compassion. I grew up ranking sins and learning to be offended by the things I thought were the worst. I am so very grateful that in my own brokenness, Jesus has stripped from me the judgment my old nature could have given. What I know today is that we both need Jesus, His grace, His mercy, and especially His strength.

The Bible teaches that in Christ we are all new creatures. I'm so thankful that we don't have to label ourselves as liars, gluttons, gossips, or thieves. Because of Jesus, you and I are new creatures who will still struggle with temptation on this earth. Yours is homosexuality, mine might be insecurity, and the person in the pew next to me at church may struggle with temptations of pornography or drug addiction or rage. But because of Christ—oh, hallelujah!—we do not have to wear the labels of our sin. I do not, and neither do you.

Even though we may never meet, can I make you a promise? From far away, I am standing with you in prayer and standing beside you in the pursuit of purity and godliness. I don't want you to think for a minute that you are alone. Somebody in this world cares, and even more, Jesus, our compassionate Savior, stands with you as the most powerful source of strength and healing. I pray you know His presence.

You are a very brave man to write the story of your private struggle. You are also obviously a very strong man to have stood in the face of such great temptation without having acted out. May your inner man continue to be strengthened by the filling of the Holy Spirit. May you increase in godliness, wisdom, and grace. I pray that the freedom of being strong in Christ will be the freedom you enjoy all the days of your life.

I am asking God to send a ministry team to help you, to surround you, to guide you, to be strong when you are weak…to be like Jesus to you.

You may be anonymous, but today, you are not alone. You are loved and prayed for, my friend.

52

THE END OR ONLY
THE BEGINNING?

From Kristen...

I am an unloved, cast out, and forgotten foster girl whose life never was like the lives of the kids I grew up with. I turn 18 in two months and age out of foster care, still with no parents or family to love. I accepted Christ when I was young, but this year was a turning point in my faith. I realized that all I really need is God. Even though I never had a father, He is my Father. I believe with all my heart that He has redeemed my life for victory and beauty.

My life is still lonely sometimes, but I love this verse: "Be strong and courageous. Do not be afraid; do not be discouraged, for the LORD your God will be with you wherever you go" (Joshua 1:9). It reminds me every day that when Jesus died on Calvary, I gained a best friend beyond any earthly ones. My story is extreme and painful, but because of what God has done for me I have healing and I have *hope*! I am now spreading that same hope to friends and fellow teens in the same boat as me, people who need to know they are loved. Jesus turned me into a princess, and now I am living out my duties till I reach my kingdom above.

"I know the plans I have for you," declares the LORD, *"plans to prosper you and not to harm you, plans to give you hope and a future"* (Jeremiah 29:11).

Matthew Responds...

The New Testament is filled with stories of people who came to Jesus. The blind, the rich, the crippled, the tax collector...You name it—when they heard Jesus was nearby, they made a beeline in His direction. Even if He was somewhere far off, people would travel great distances and go through great lengths to meet this man who was the promised Messiah. And why? Well, on the surface, they all came for different reasons.

- The paralytic's friends lowered him through the roof in hope that he could walk again (Luke 5:17-26).
- The sick woman who had been bleeding for 12 years crawled through a crowd to Jesus in hope that she would be healed (Mark 5:25-34).
- The leper came to Jesus in hope of being made clean (Matthew 8:1-4).
- The demon-possessed came to Jesus in hope of being freed (Matthew 8:28-34).
- Mary and Martha sent word to Jesus in hope that their brother, Lazarus, would be healed (John 11:1-44).

Yes, on the surface, all of these people had different reasons for coming to Jesus. But they all shared a common drive that drew them to the feet of a Savior: Each one knew exactly where he or she was in life and was not content to stay there. They each believed that Jesus could lift them to where they wanted to be. Instead of just resigning themselves to their current circumstances, their current state of pain, and their current lot in life, they made their way to the One they heard could show them something better.

In reading all of these biblical stories, you will notice that not once did these people hesitate to ask Jesus for help. Nowhere does it say that when Bartimaeus, the blind man, heard Jesus of Nazareth was walking by, he contemplated whether he should even give it a shot. The guy had been blind his whole life, for all we know. You would think by that time in his life, he may have had this mind-set: "This is about the best I'm gonna do. I started my life blind, and I'll end my life blind." But instead, "When he heard that it was Jesus of Nazareth, he began shouting, 'Jesus, Son of David, have mercy on me!'" (Mark 10:47). See, Bartimaeus was well aware of his circumstances, but he was still full of hope at the mention of Jesus' name. He believed that his life could become something more than what he had known—and he was right. "'Go,' said Jesus, 'your faith has healed you.'"

Are you surrounded by a set of circumstances that leaves you feeling resigned to think your life is just the way it will always be? Perhaps you can relate to Kristen's story—a rocky childhood and no family to love. You've been handed a part of your story that you didn't ask for and certainly would never wish for. Kristen didn't ask to be abandoned by her family. She didn't choose to be passed around from one foster home to the next. No child wishes for these things, and no child should ever have to experience that level of abandonment.

Kristen might have decided that since she never had known love, she never would. But Kristen refused to give up that quickly. She made the choice to follow the same trail blazed by Bartimaeus and all the others. She came to Jesus, placing her hurtful childhood in His hands, and discovered the promise of a greater love than she had ever known before.

I remember speaking with Kristen for the first time on the phone. I was about to play her the song her story inspired when she said to me, "You know, I just began to realize that even though my life has really stunk so far, it isn't over. I now see that it's really just beginning!" I sat for a moment on the other end of the line, stunned because of the first line of the song I had written for her: "Is this the end or only the beginning?"

Kristen had not even heard her song yet! That was definitely a special moment I won't soon forget, a moment that proved to me that

God was going to use Kristen's story in a powerful way. And He is. Kristen is now living her life determined to be the proof that our broken beginnings can become beautiful stories of God's redemption when we simply come to Jesus. Wherever you are today, ask yourself this question: Is this the end, or only the beginning? Kristen knows the answer to that question, and she's just getting started.

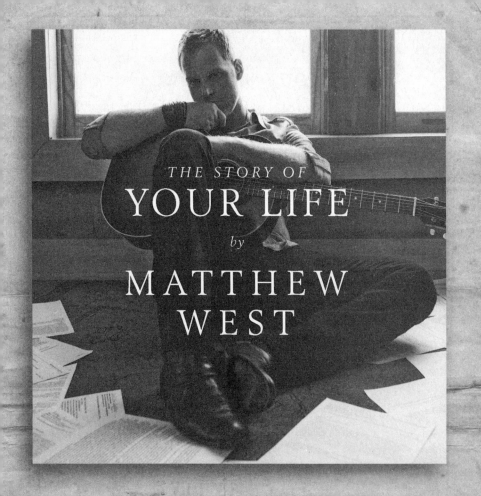

THE STORY OF
YOUR LIFE
by
MATTHEW
WEST

THE NEW ALBUM
INSPIRED BY OVER 10,000
REAL-LIFE STORIES

features
MY OWN LITTLE WORLD
STRONG ENOUGH

Available Now

SPARROW®

www.matthewwest.com | *www.sparrowrecords.com*

ABOUT MATTHEW...

A pastor's son, Grammy-nominated singer-songwriter Matthew West grew up in Downers Grove, Illinois, and released three independent albums before signing to a major label and issuing his first studio album, *Happy*. The project yielded the hit "More," which topped the charts for nine weeks and became the most-played song on Christian radio in 2004. The following year, he released *History*, an acclaimed collection that included the hit title track and the instant classic "Only Grace."

After a career-threatening vocal surgery in 2007, Matthew reemerged in 2008 with *Something to Say*, serving up the memorable hits "You Are Everything" and "The Motions," which were Billboard's Most-Played Christian Songs in 2009 and 2010. "The Motions" also earned a Grammy nomination for Best Gospel Song in 2010.

His latest album, *The Story of Your Life*, was inspired by 10,000 stories from every state in the US and 20 countries. The album released in the fall of 2010 and garnered attention from CNN, Fox News, *Billboard* Magazine, *Country Weekly*, *American Songwriter*, and more. His songwriting credits include Rascal Flatts, Billy Ray Cyrus, Diamond Rio, Michael W. Smith, Mandisa, Natalie Grant, Point of Grace, and more.

Share the story of your life with Matthew at
www.matthewwest.com/story.

ALSO FROM MATTHEW WEST—
WHAT'S YOUR STORY?

...the DVD

In 2010, Grammy-nominated recording artist Matthew West stepped outside his own life and recorded an album inspired by the lives of more than 10,000 listeners who sent him their stories. Matthew was transformed by the experience, and now you can be too with the *What's Your Story? DVD*. It includes five sessions that feature teaching presentations by Matthew (set in the mountain cabin where he wrote the songs for the album), interviews from some of the people who shared their stories, and music. You will...

- discover the powerful way God uses the story of people's lives
- identify and treasure your own unique story
- compassionately embrace other people's stories

This DVD is perfect for your own use, small groups, and Sunday school settings. It's complete by itself but also corresponds with the companion book...

...the book

"The story of your life is a story worth telling," says Grammy-nominated recording artist Matthew West on his bestselling album *The Story of Your Life*. In this new book, Matthew develops that theme, showing how everyone's life is a story in progress and how knowing that truth can change people for the better.

Filled with powerful personal stories from Matthew and his fans, *What's Your Story?* is a guidebook that will help you heal from the hurts of your past and develop a deeper compassion toward others whose life stories are filled with pain. You will find that God, the author of your story, is willing and able to rewrite the broken chapters of your life.

What's Your Story? is the perfect companion to the *What's Your Story? DVD*. It includes extensive study questions for you or your small group and plenty of space for you to record your insights.